Mandala

COLORING BOOK FOR ADULT RELAXATION

Lady Melamory

This book belongs to

Lady Melamory

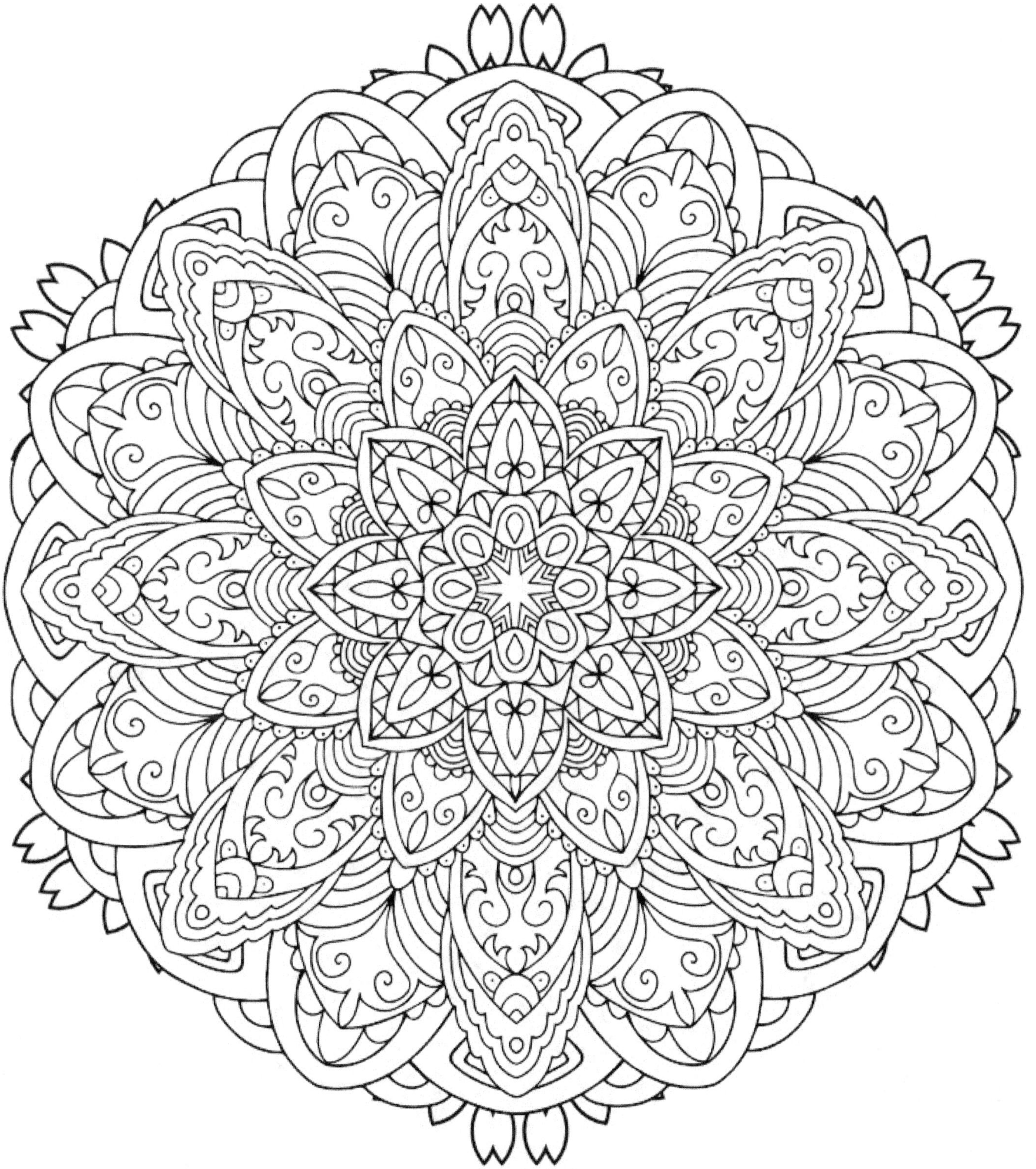

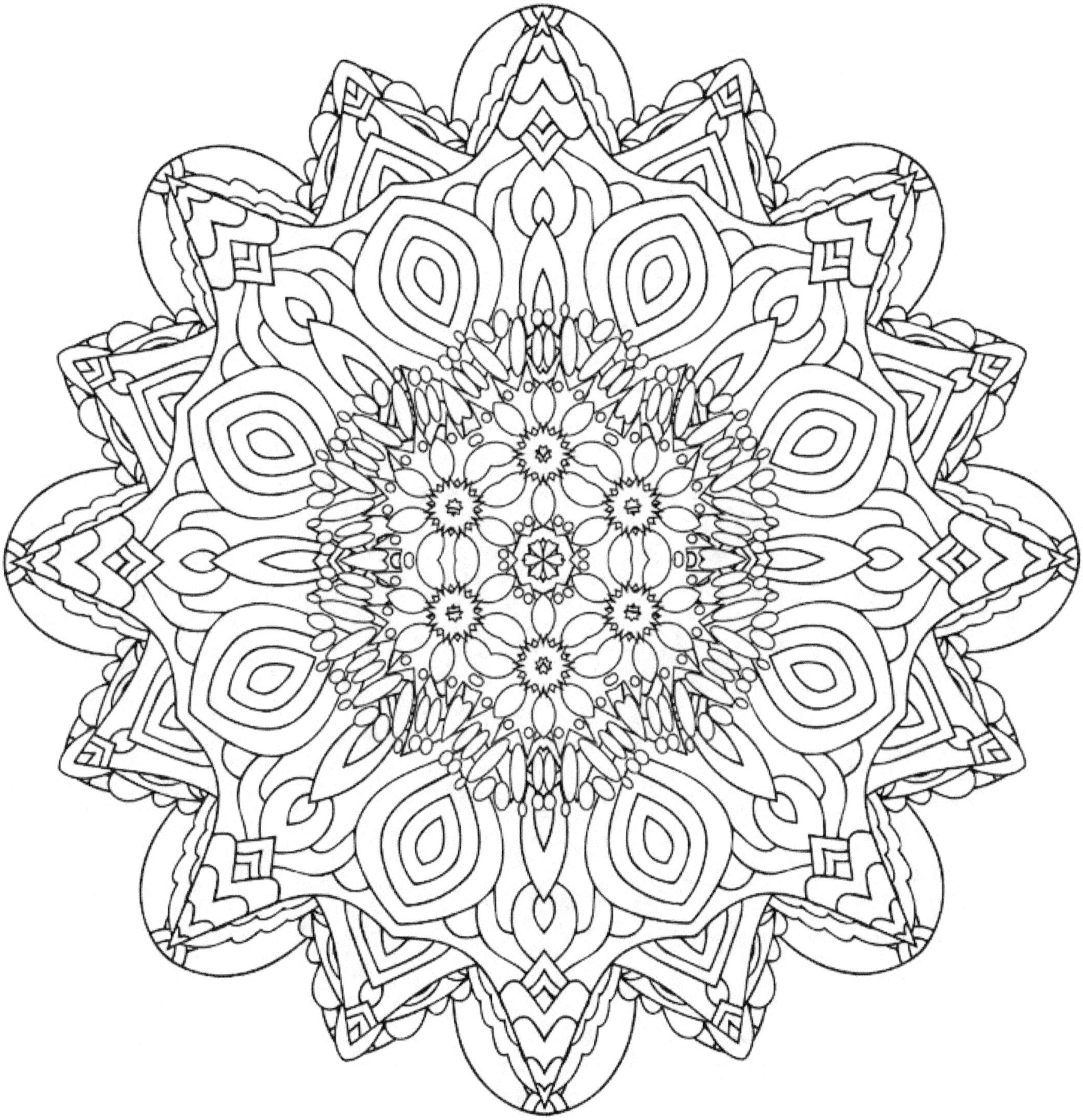

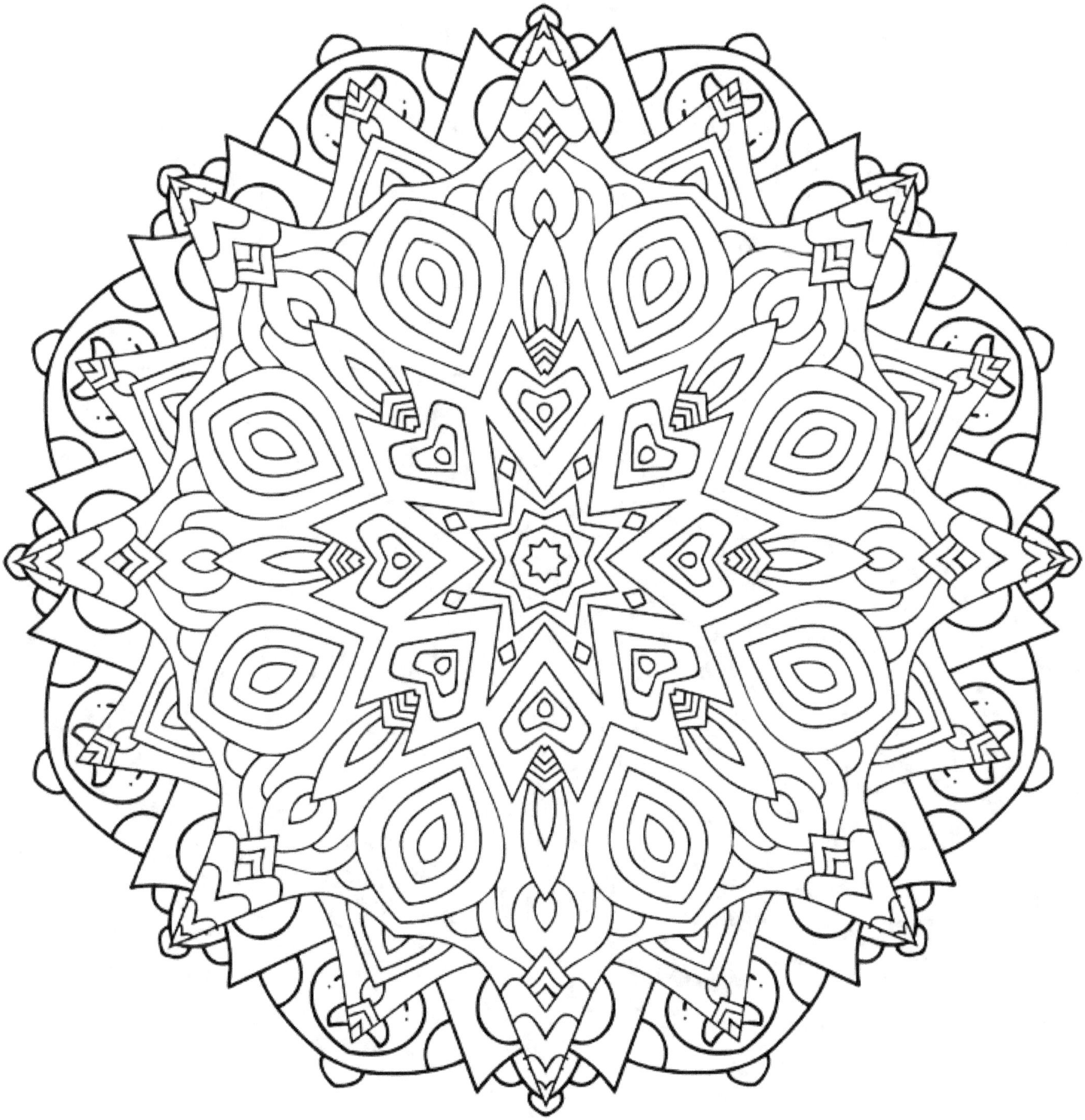

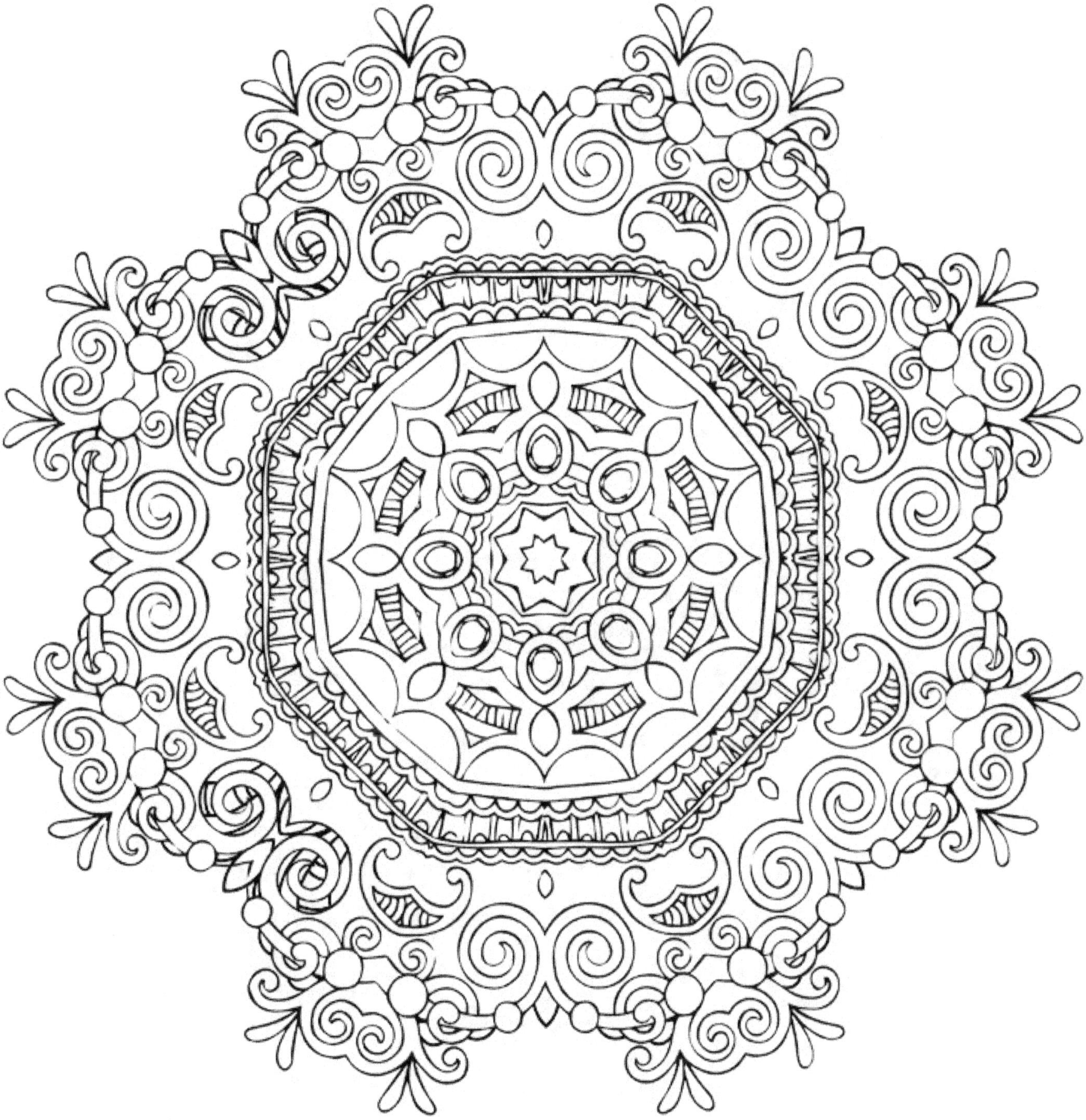

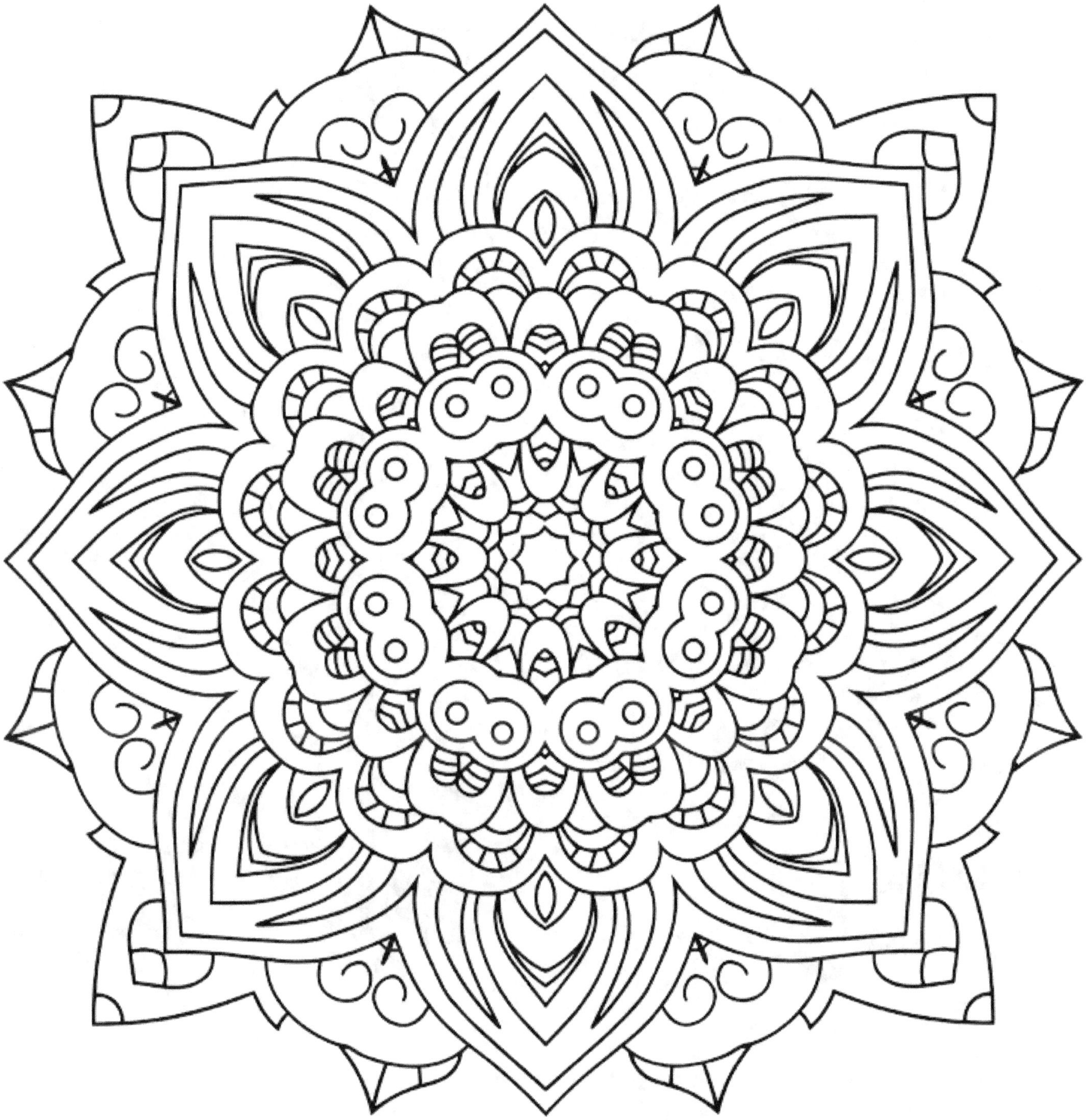

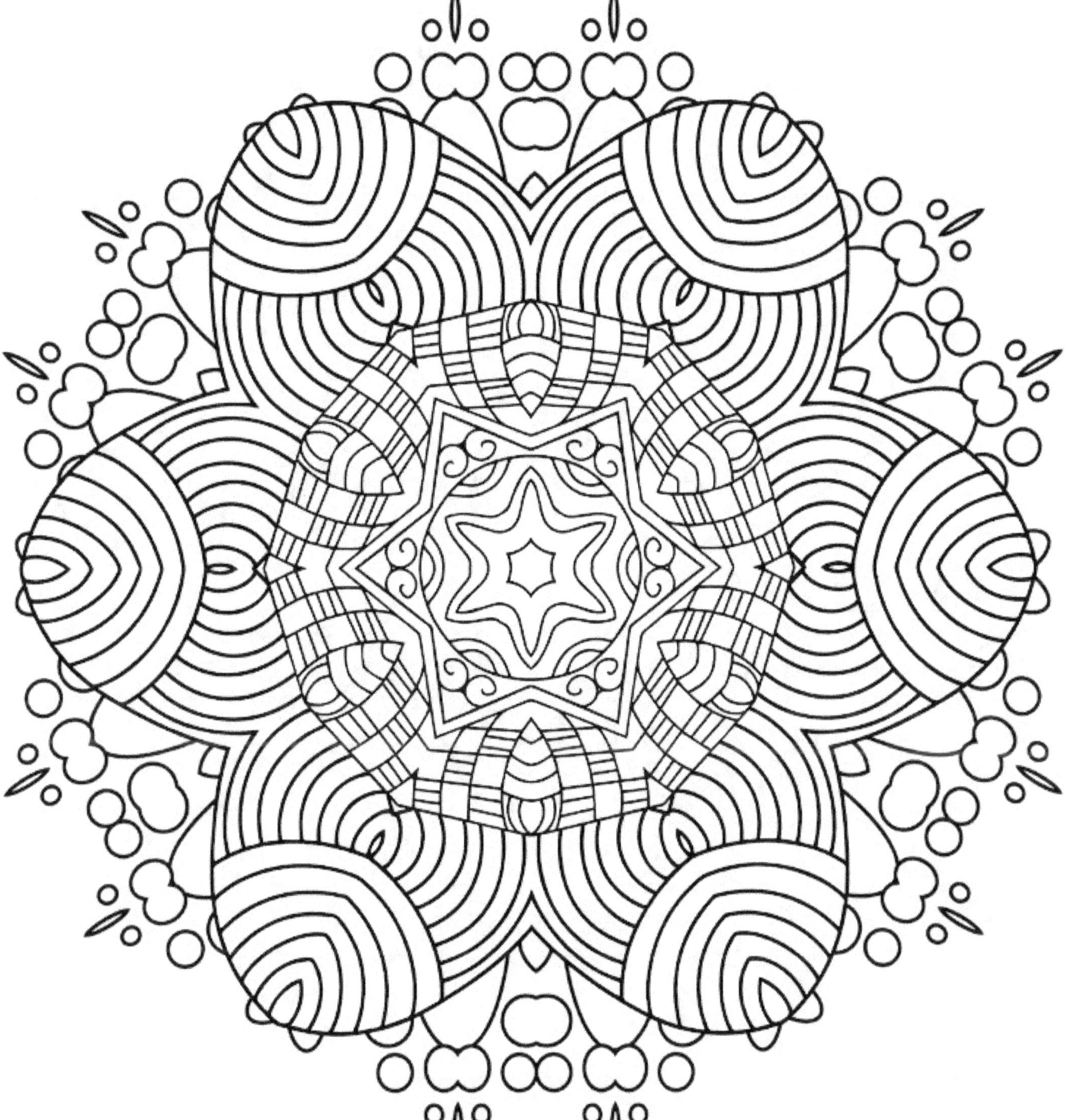

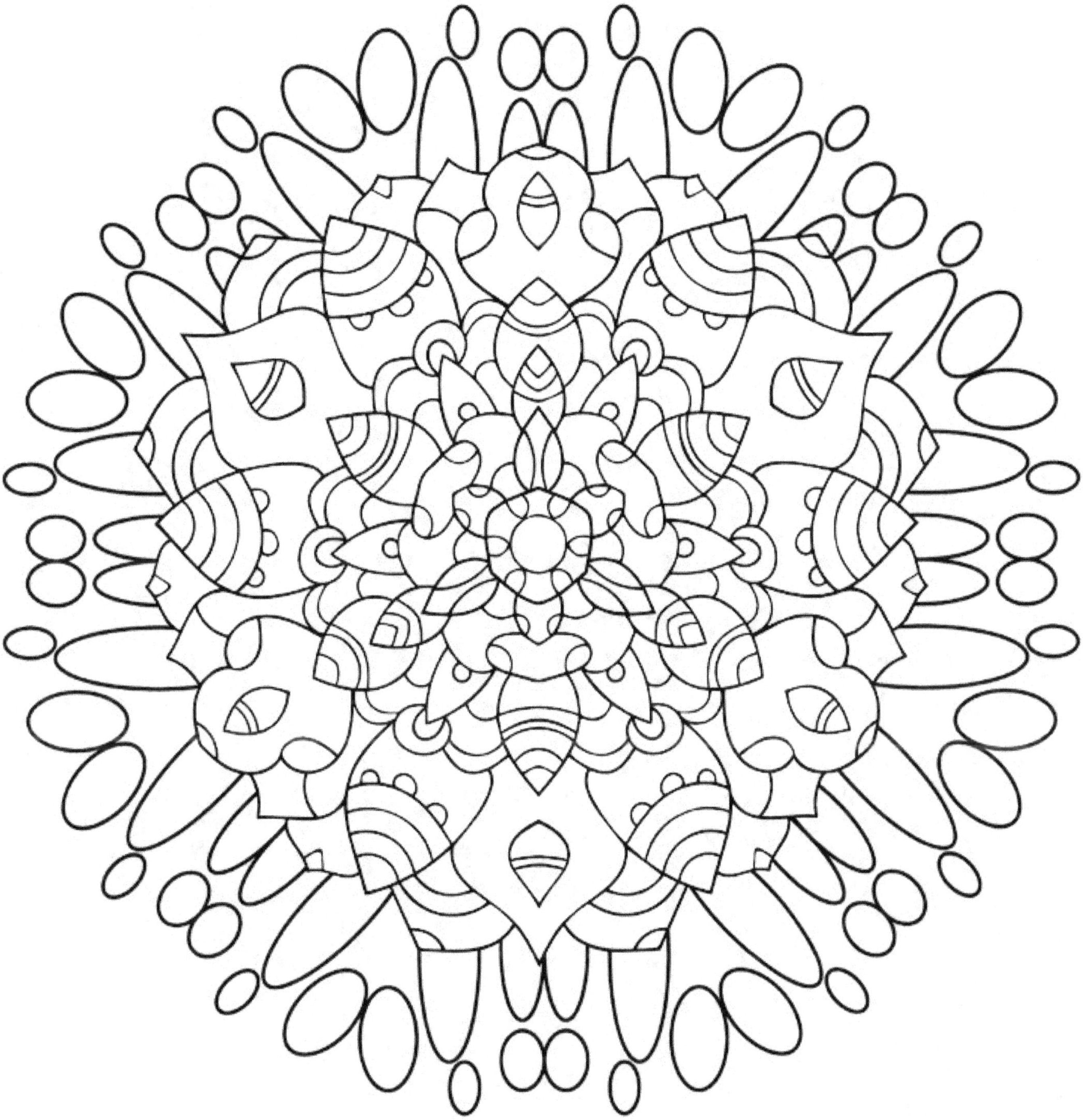

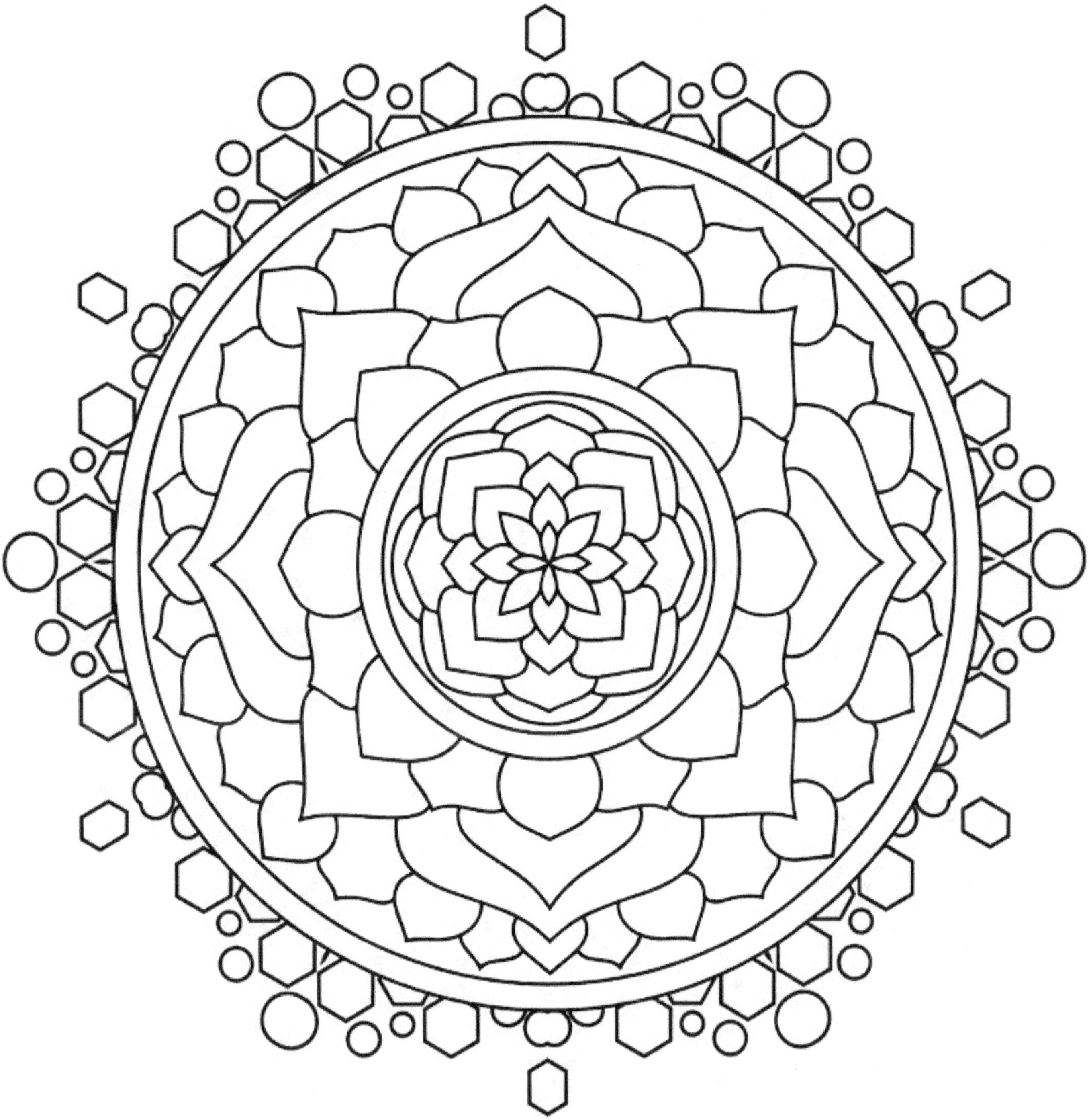

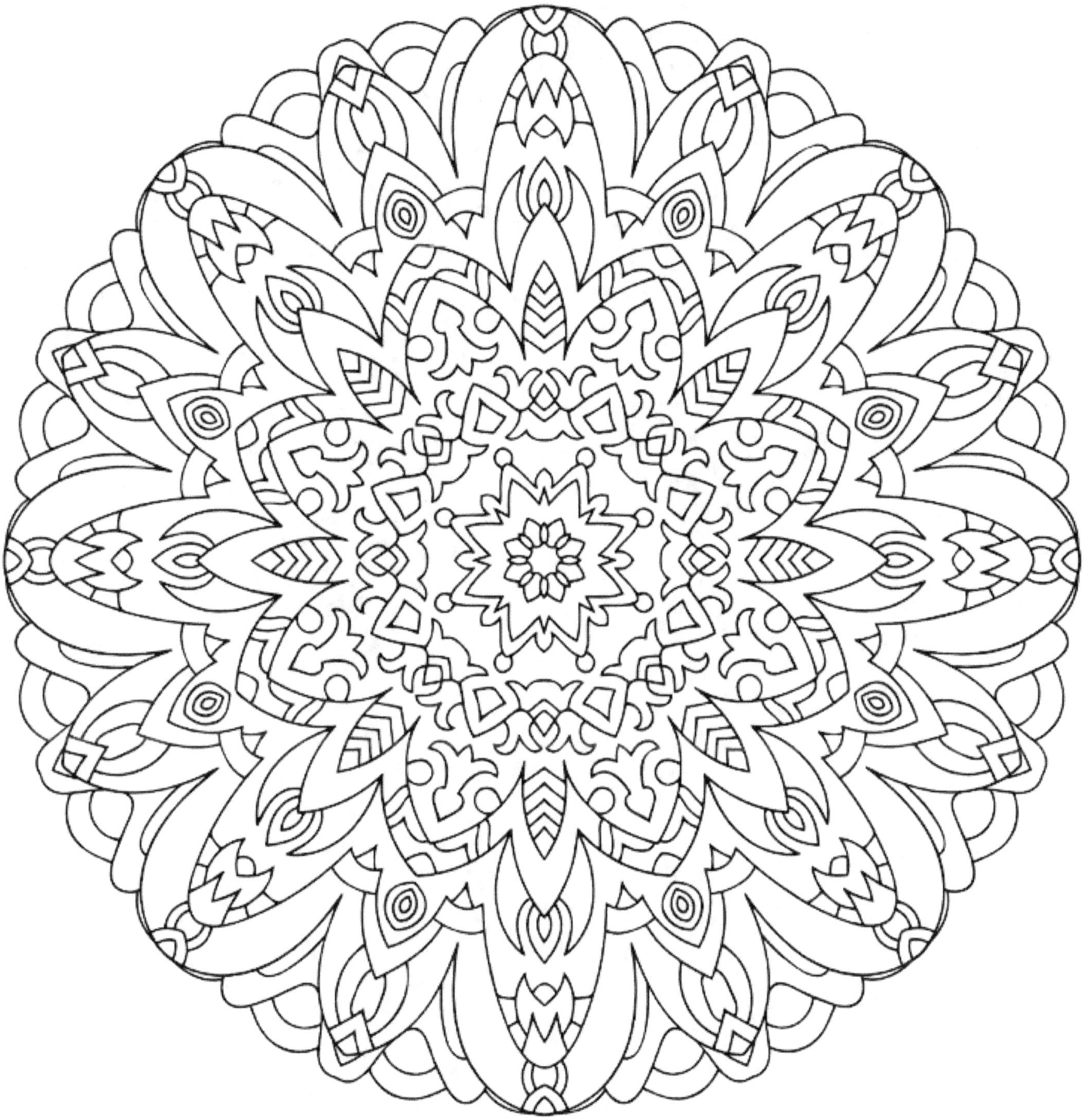

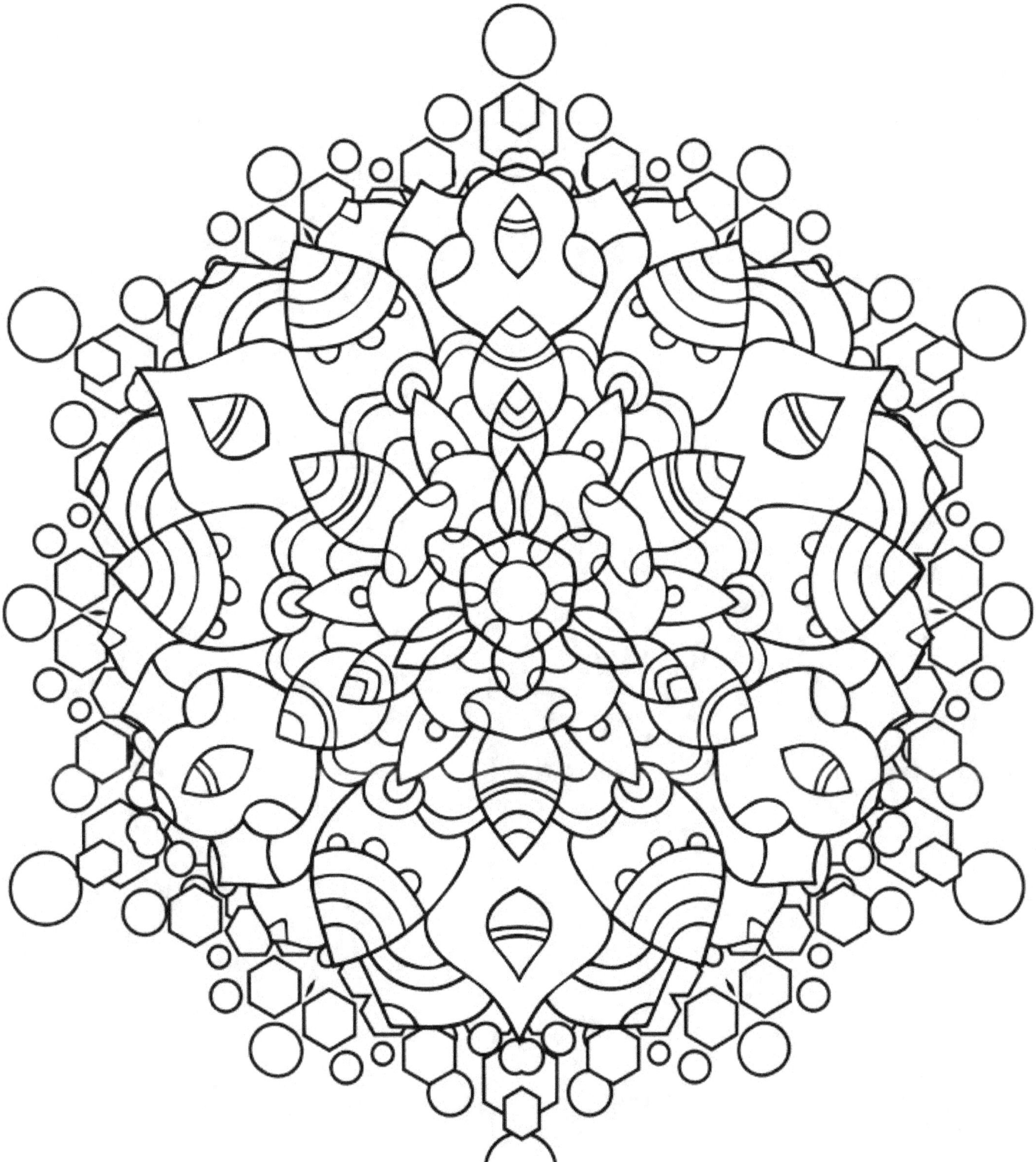

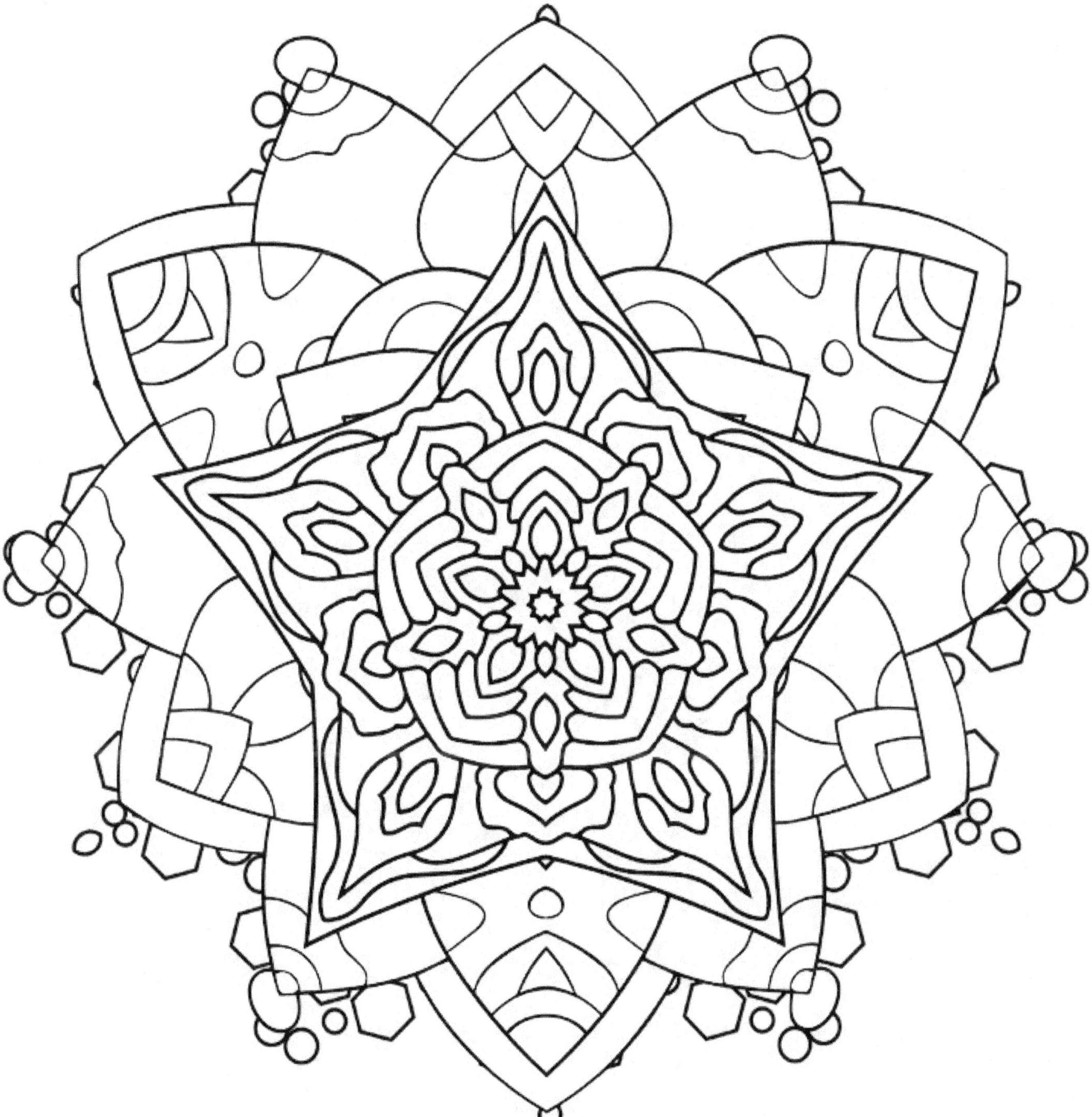

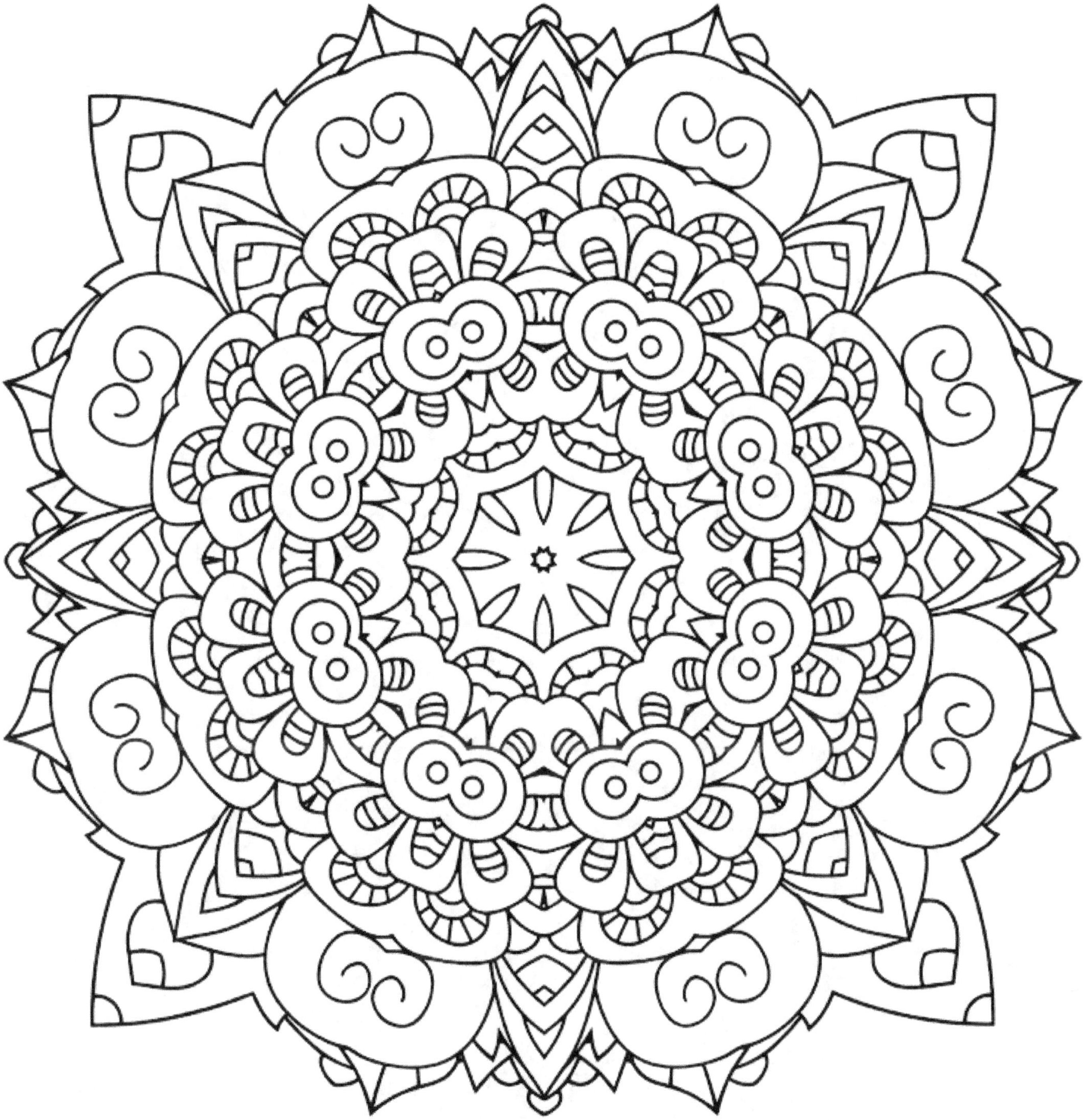

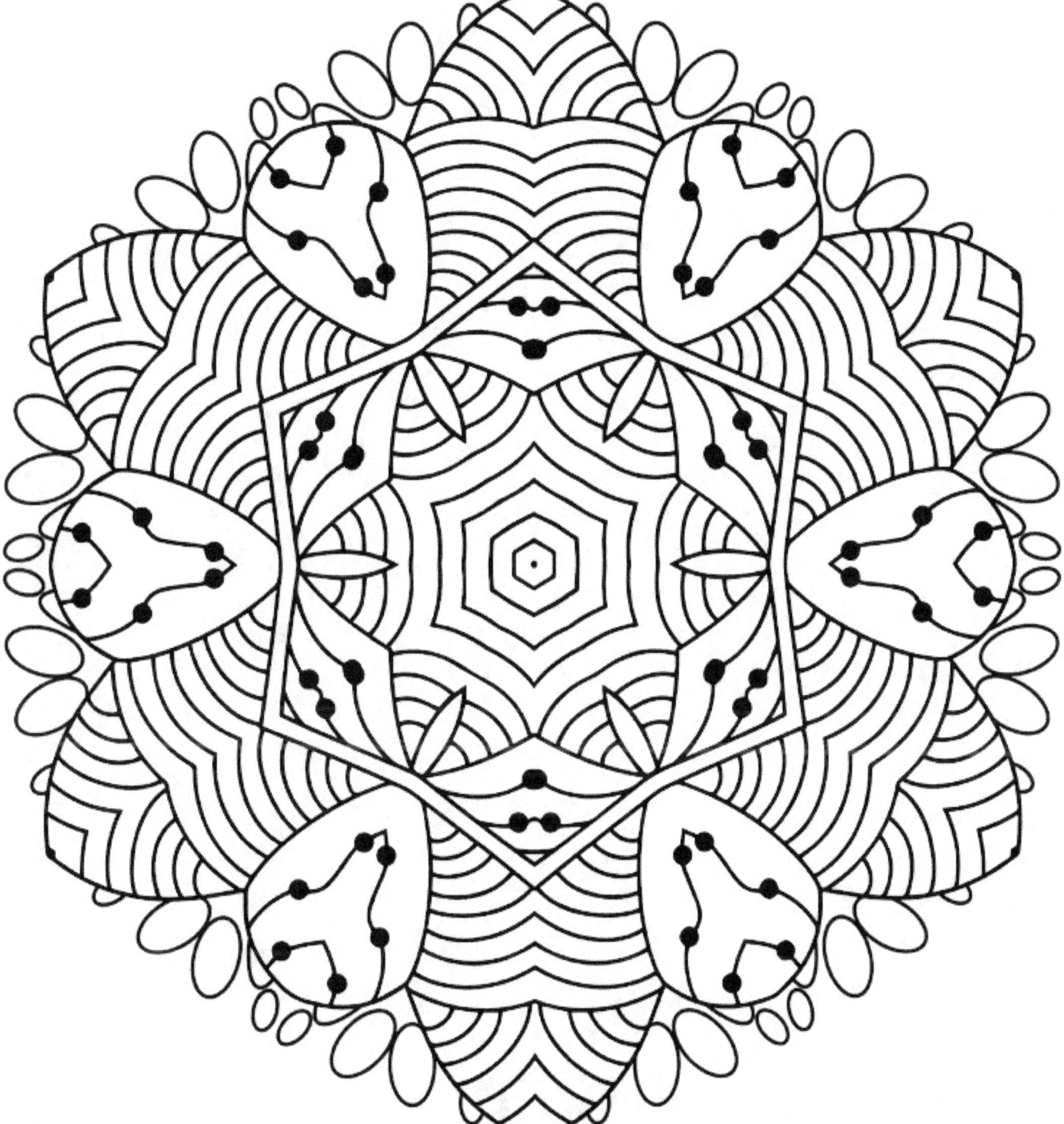

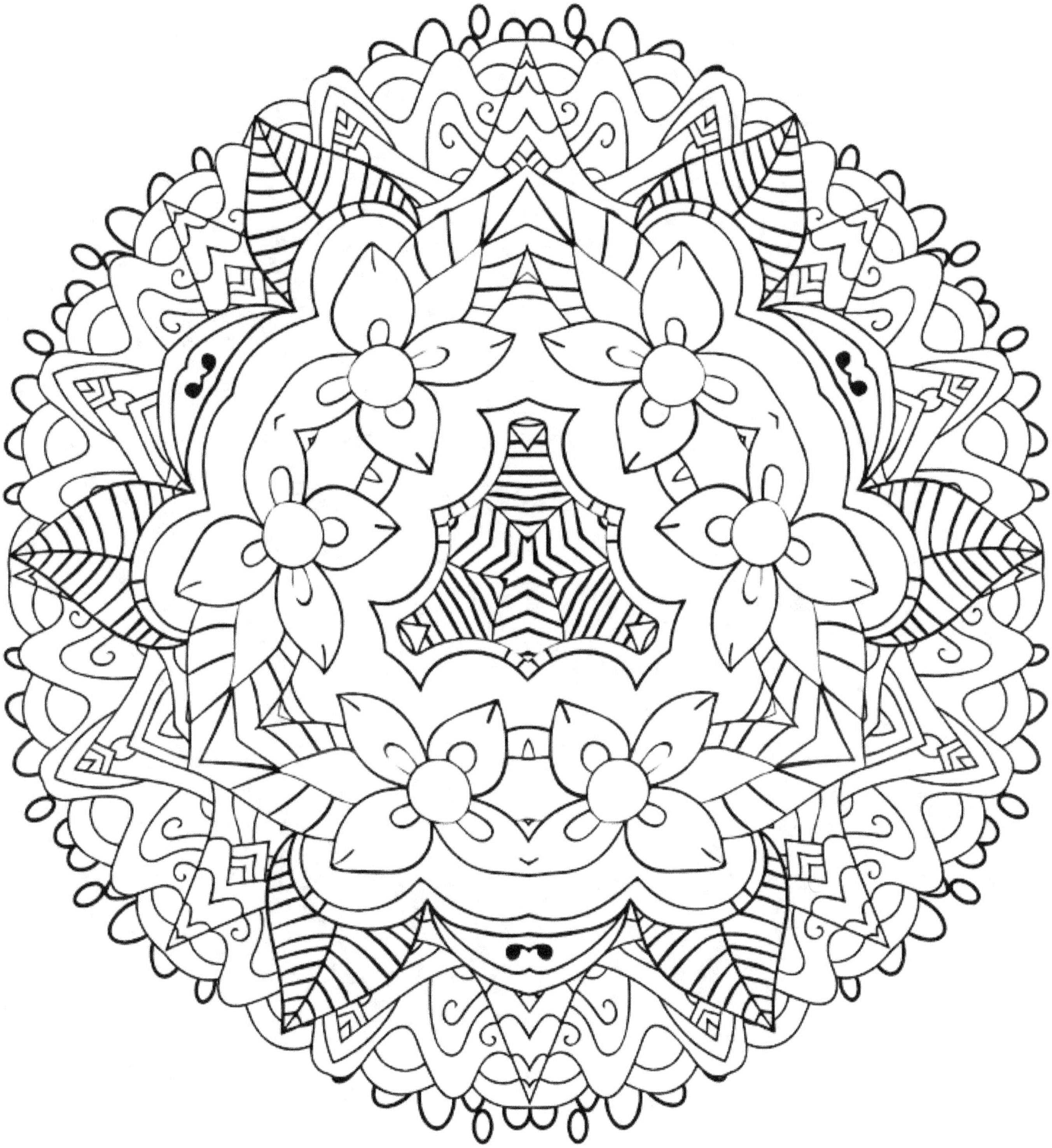

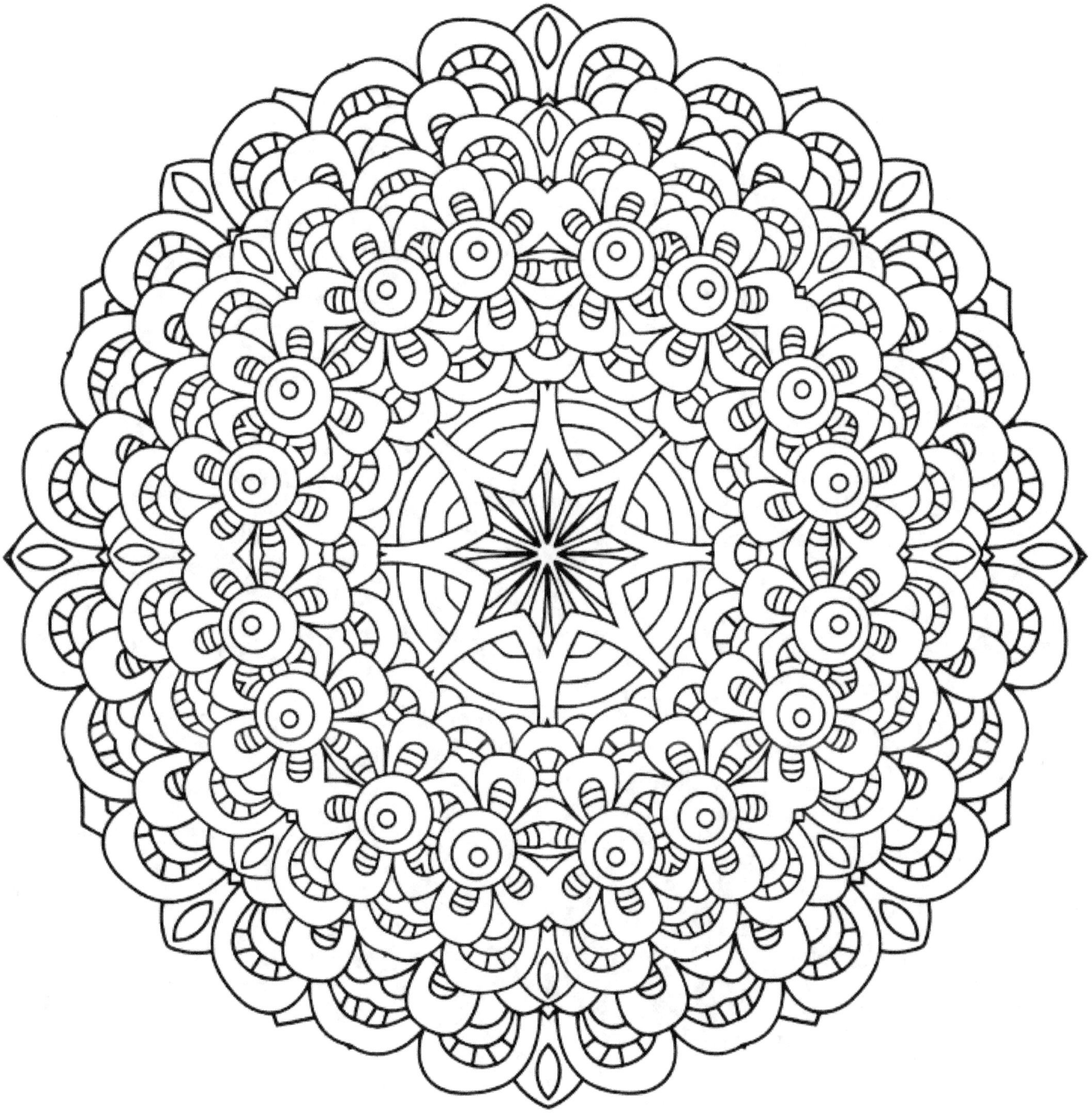

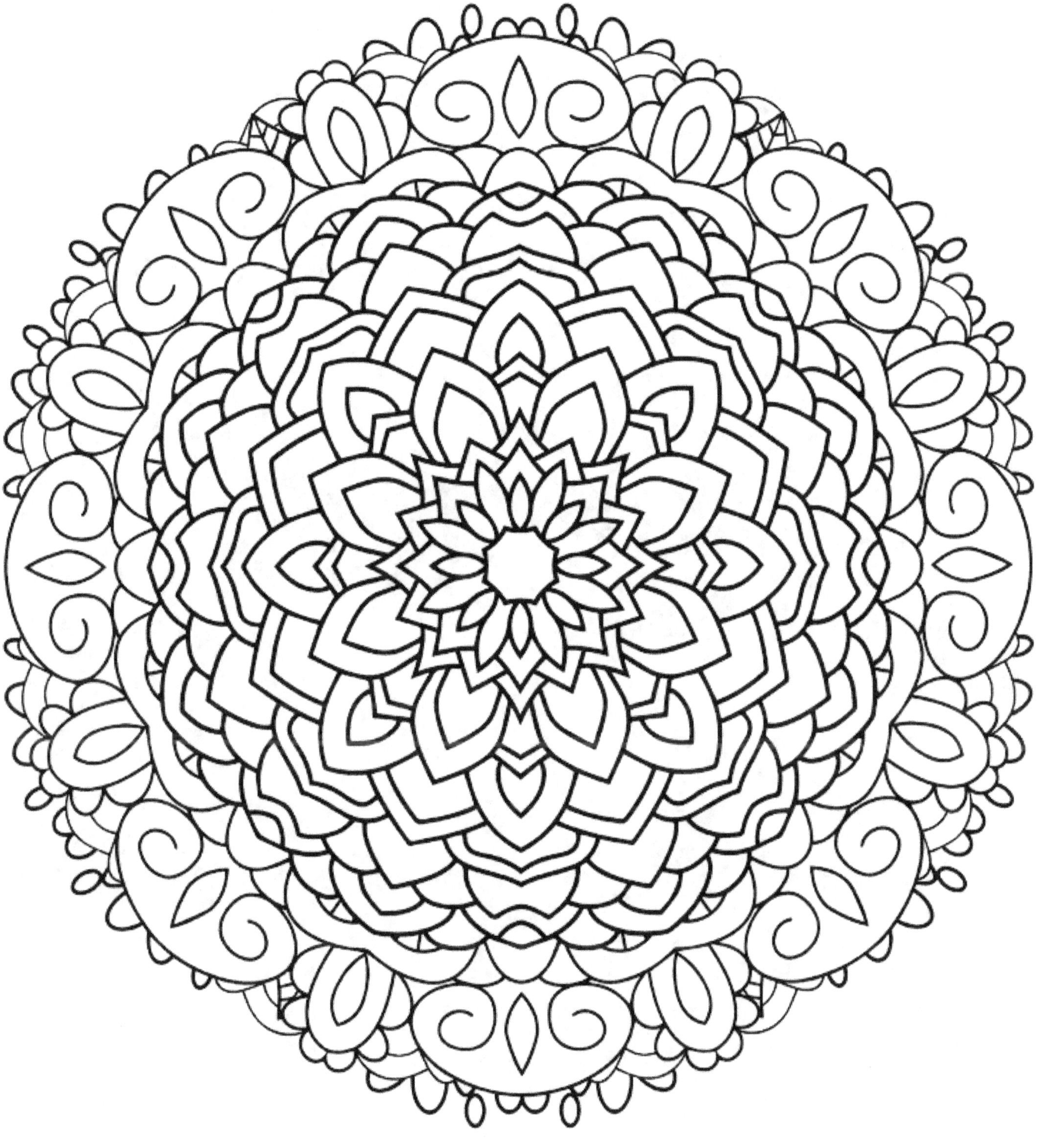

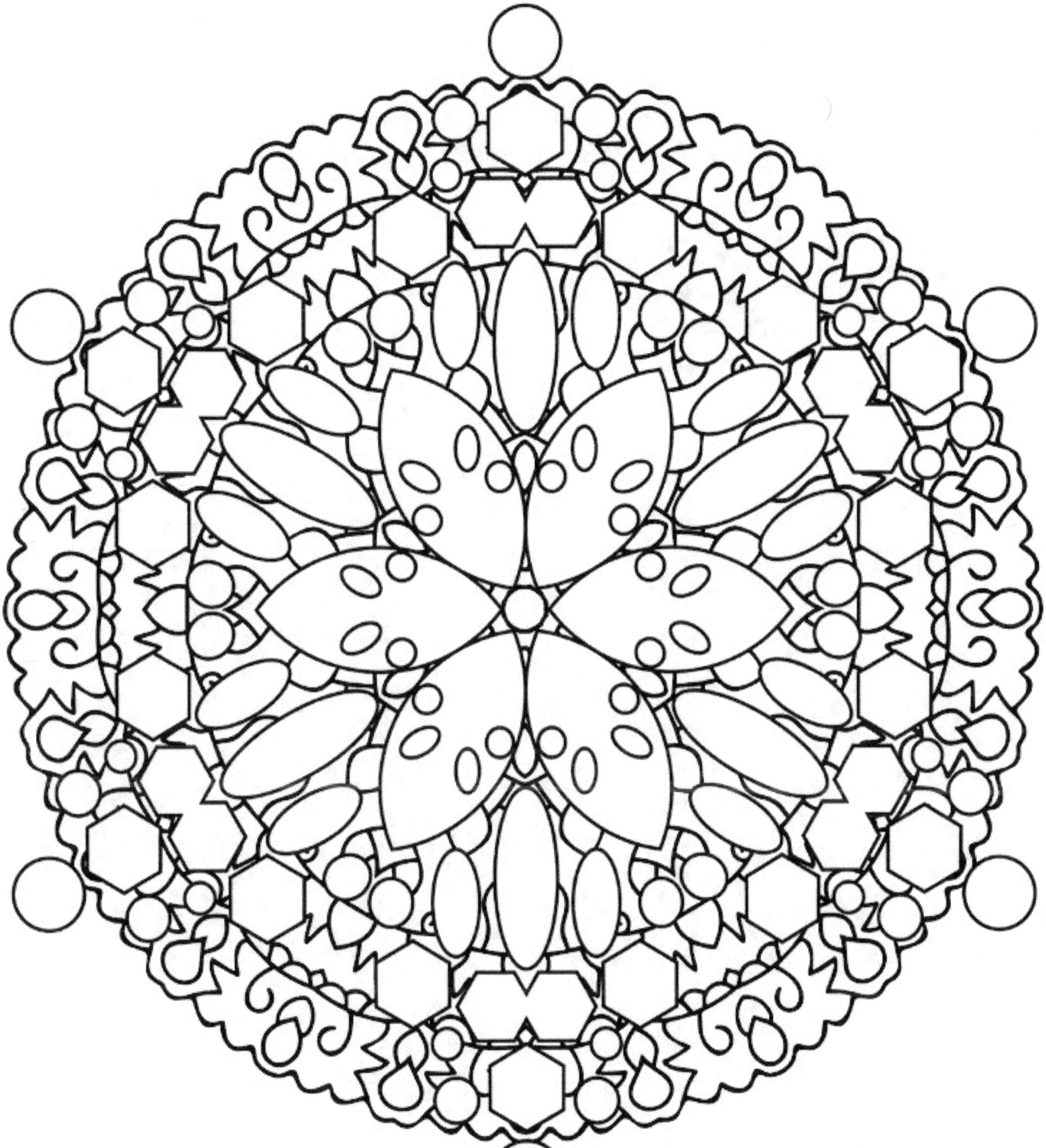

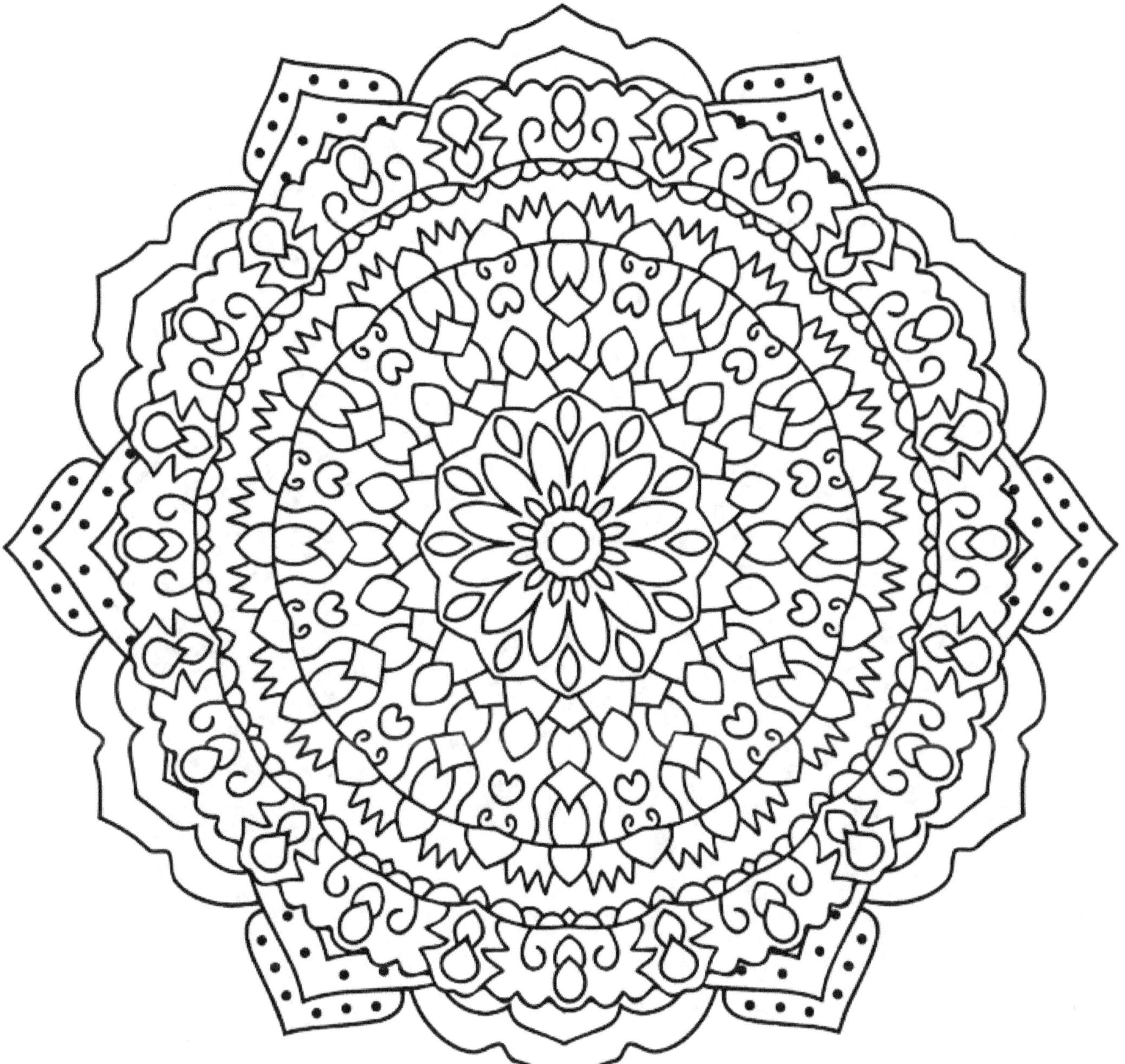

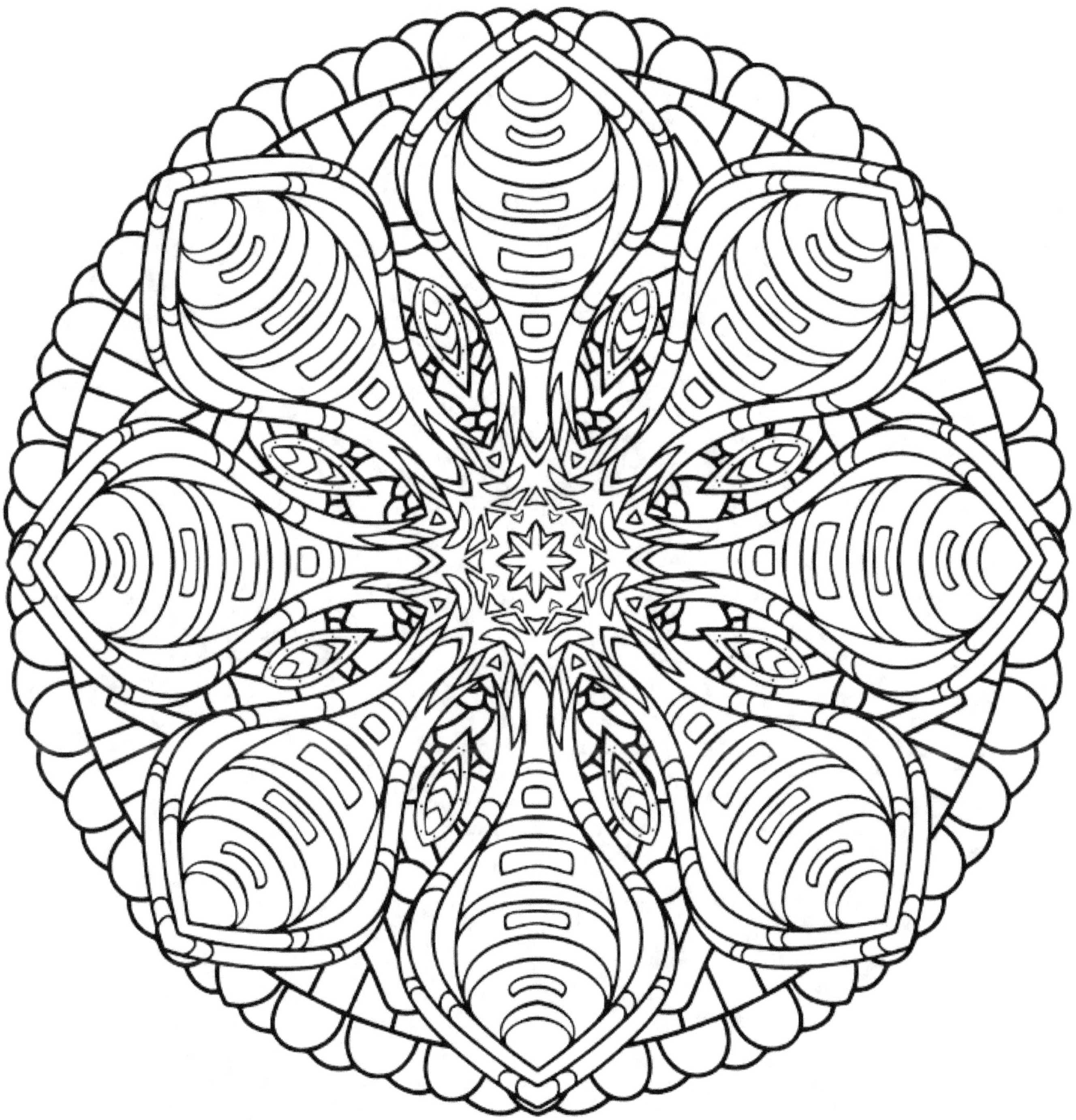

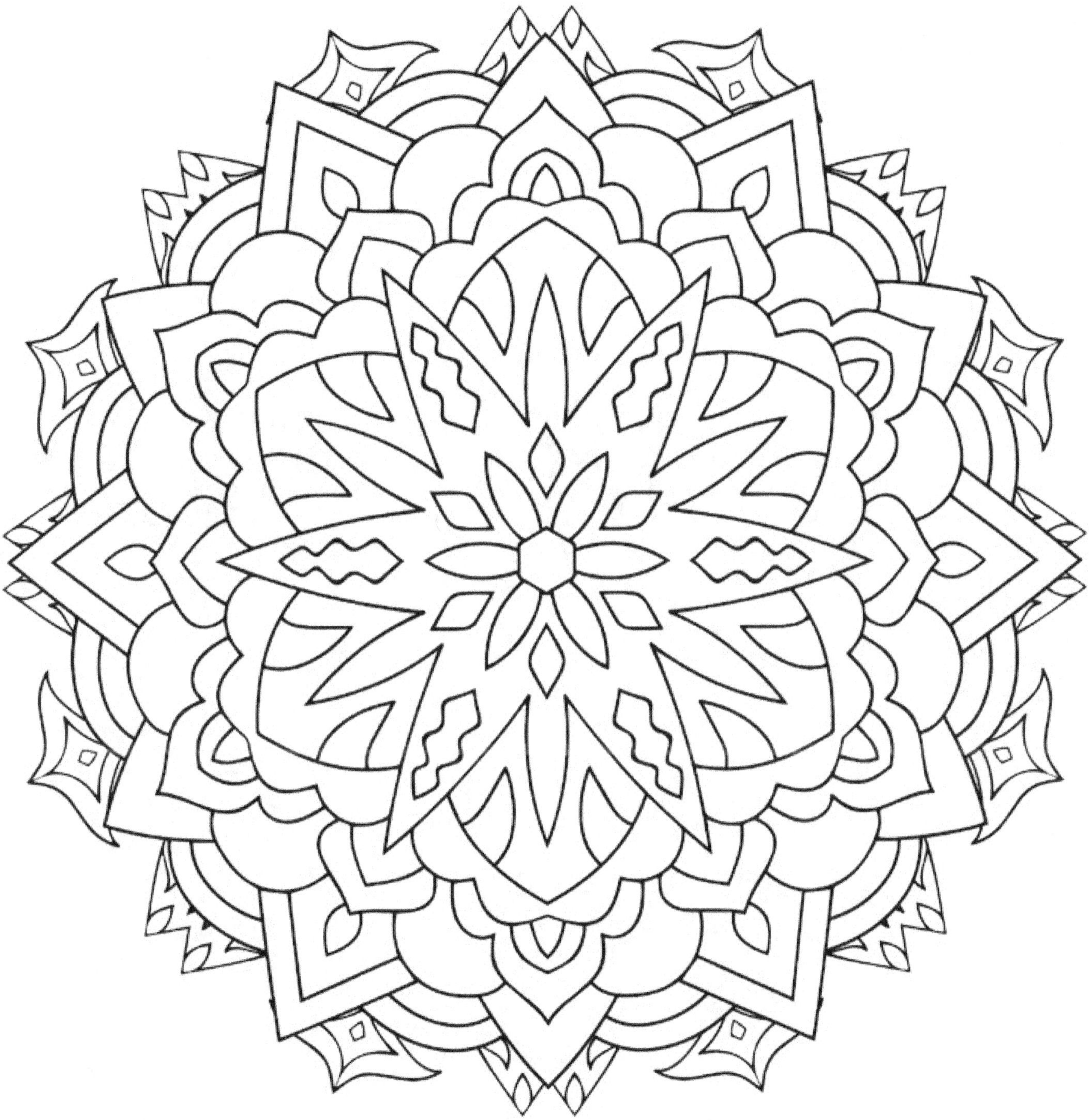

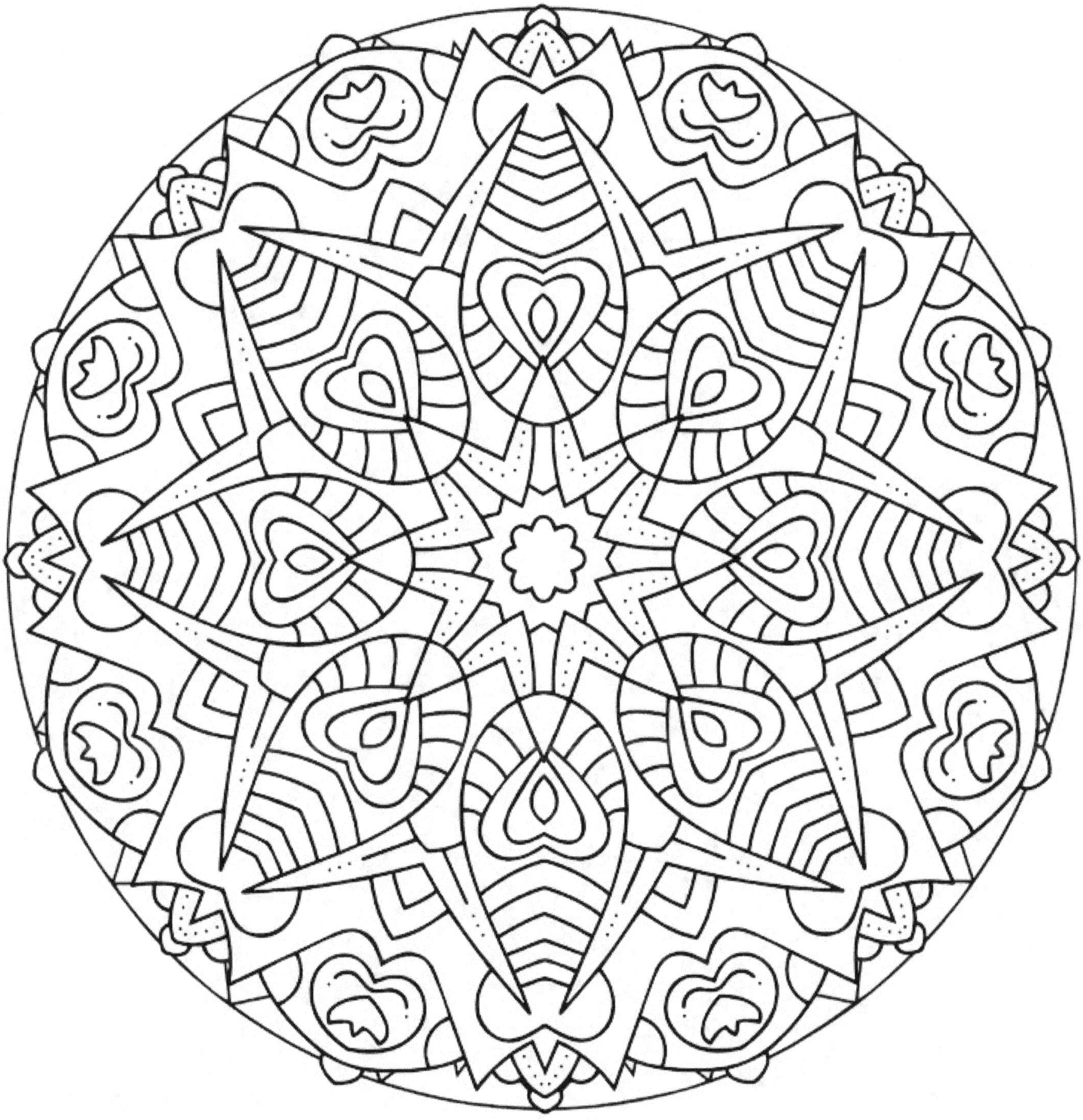

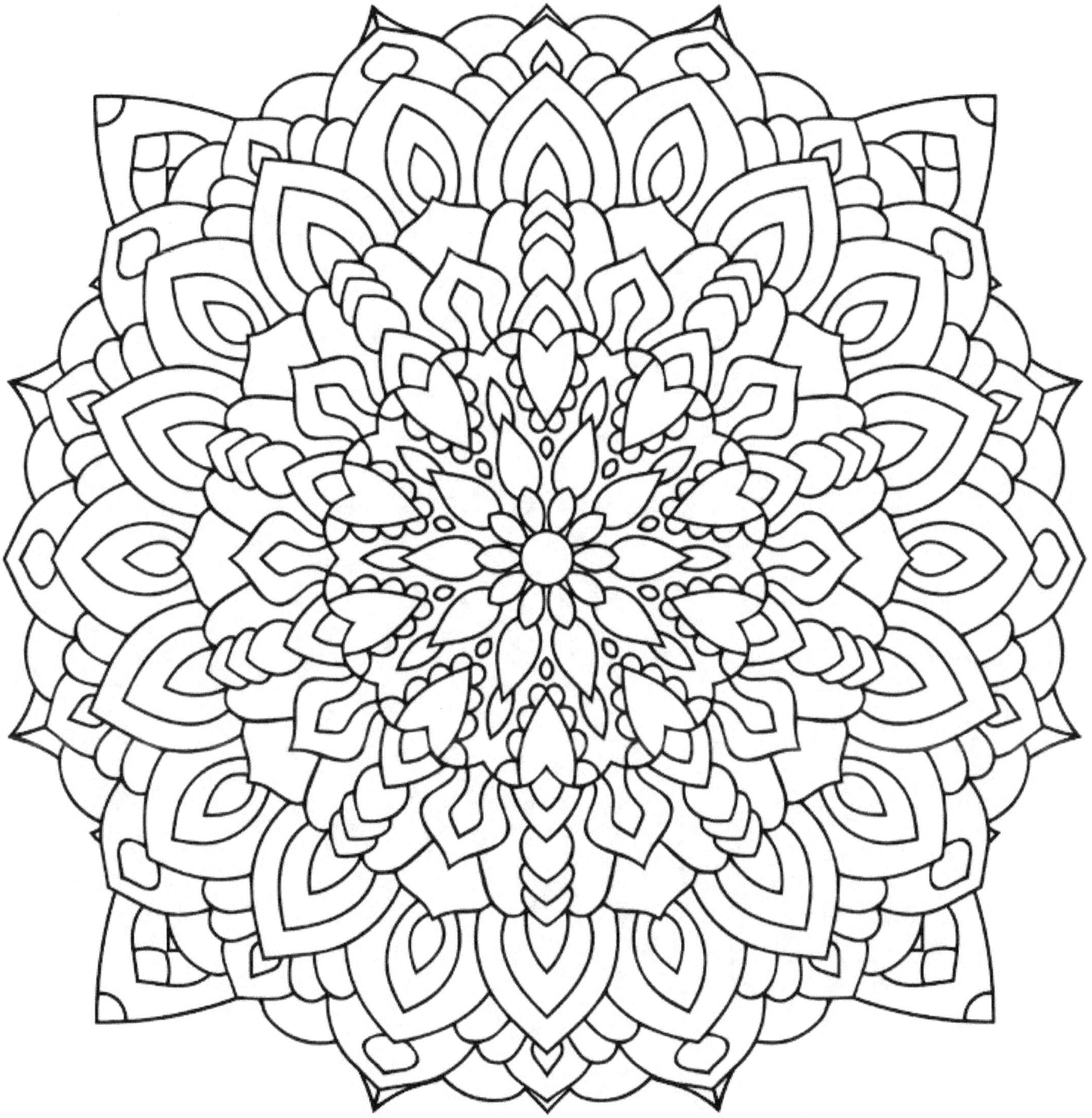

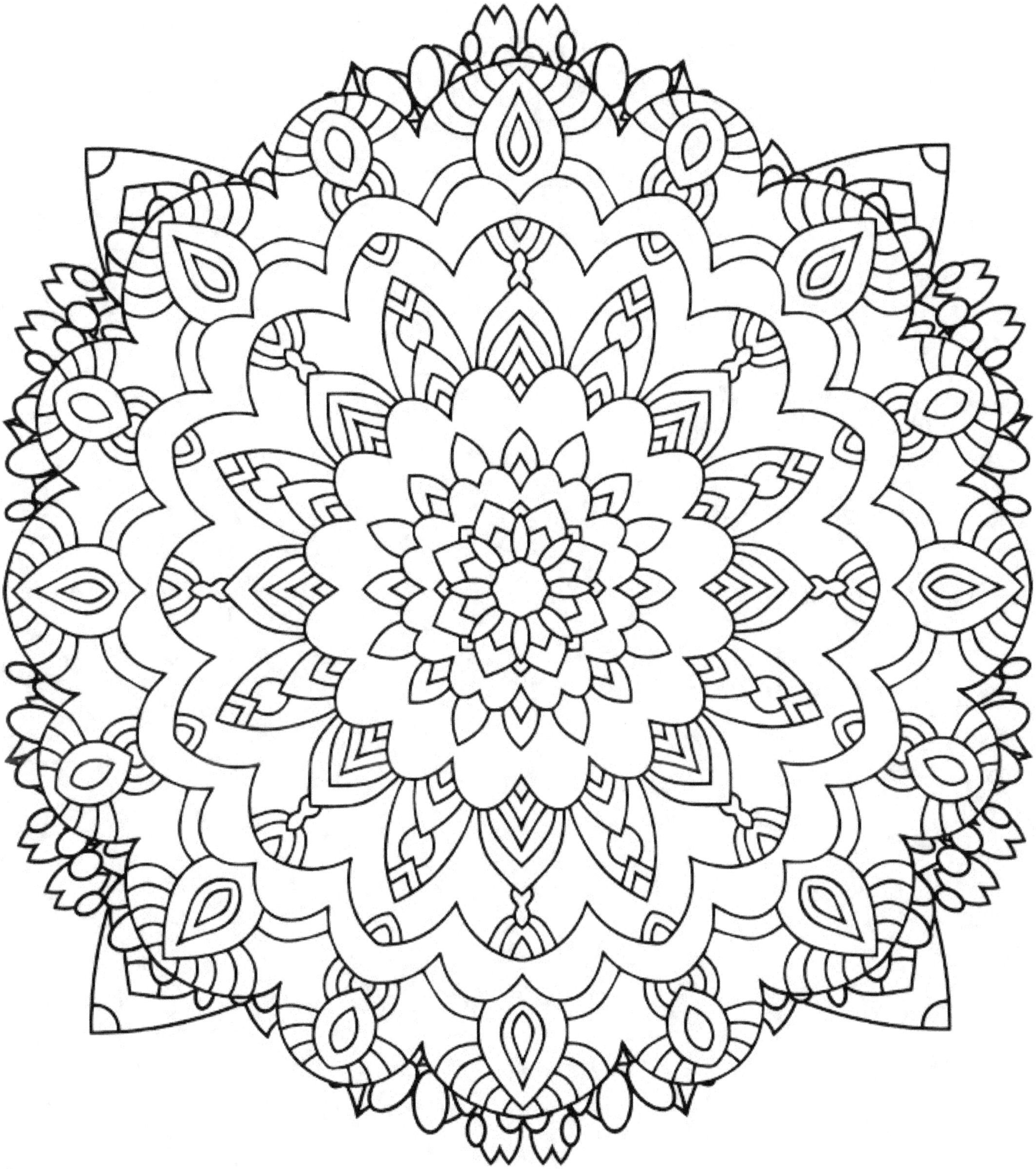

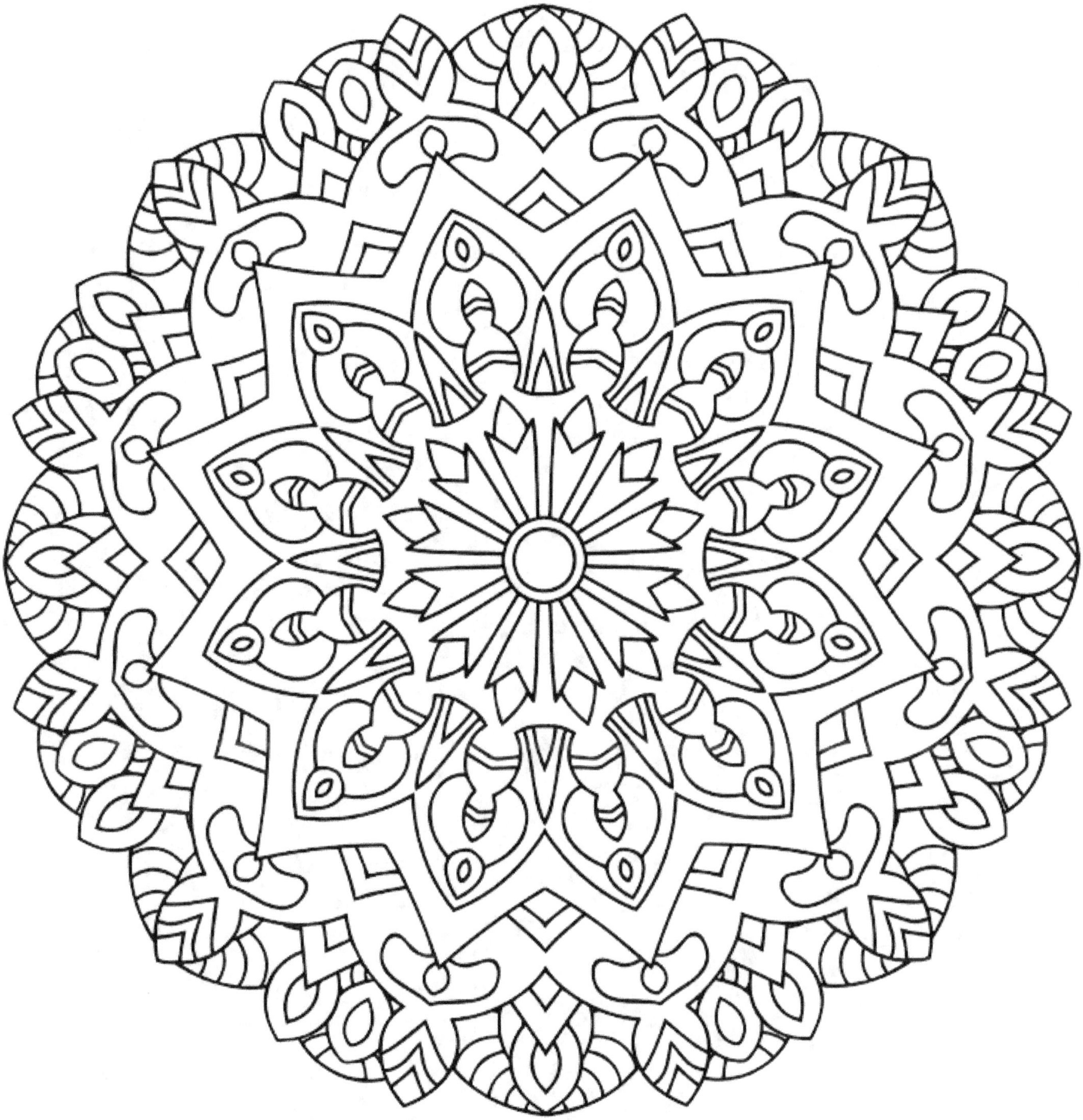

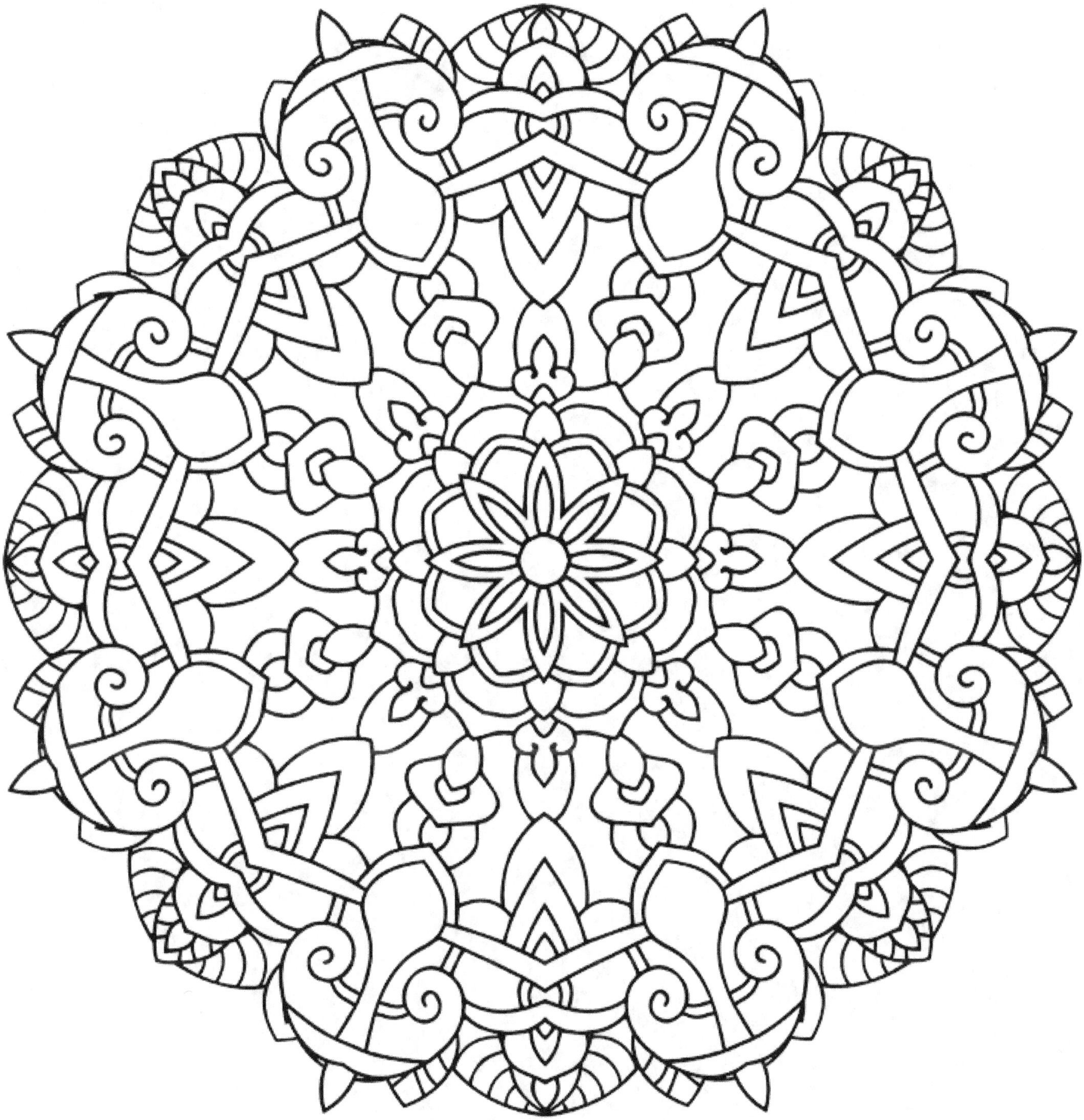

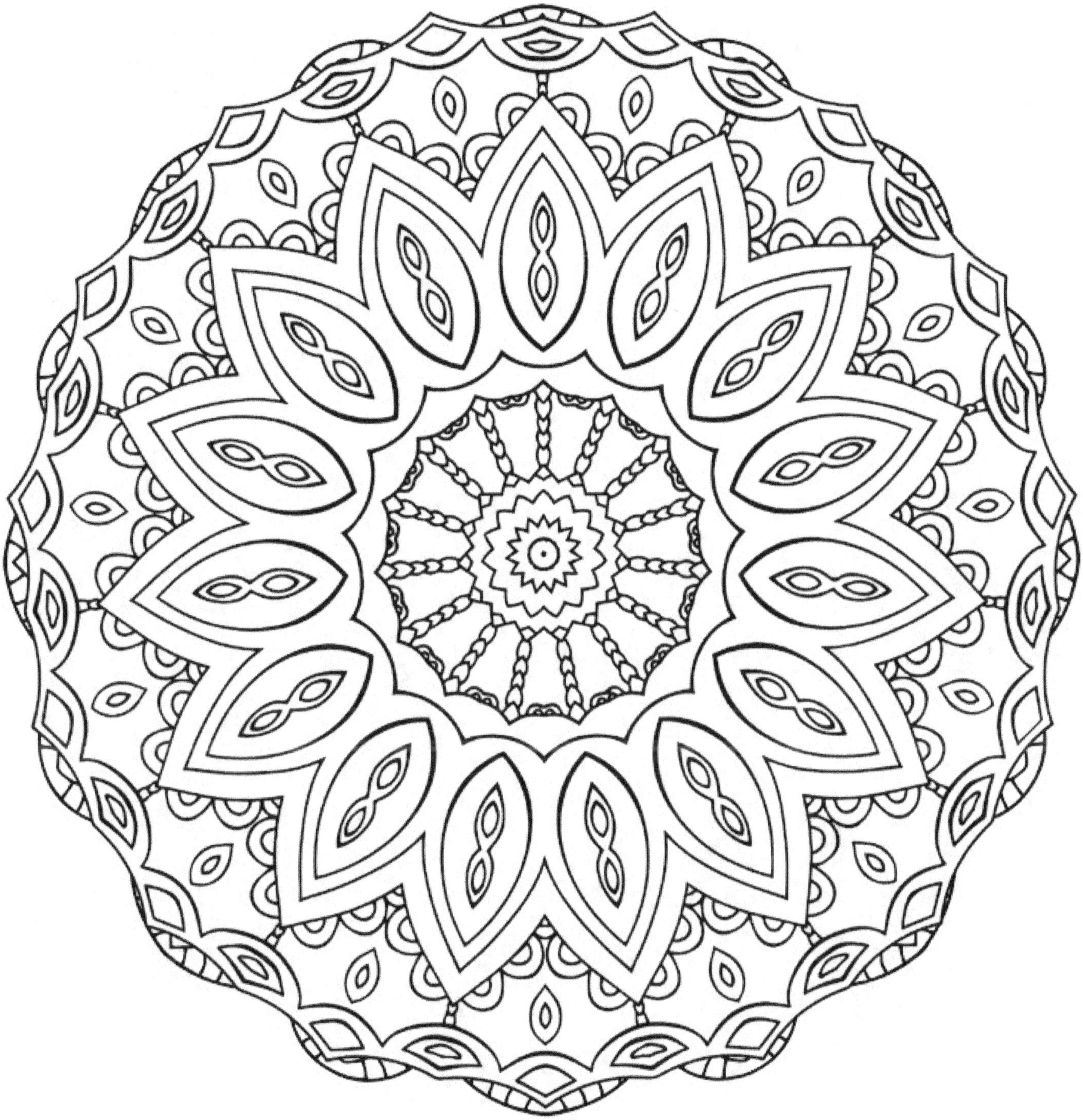

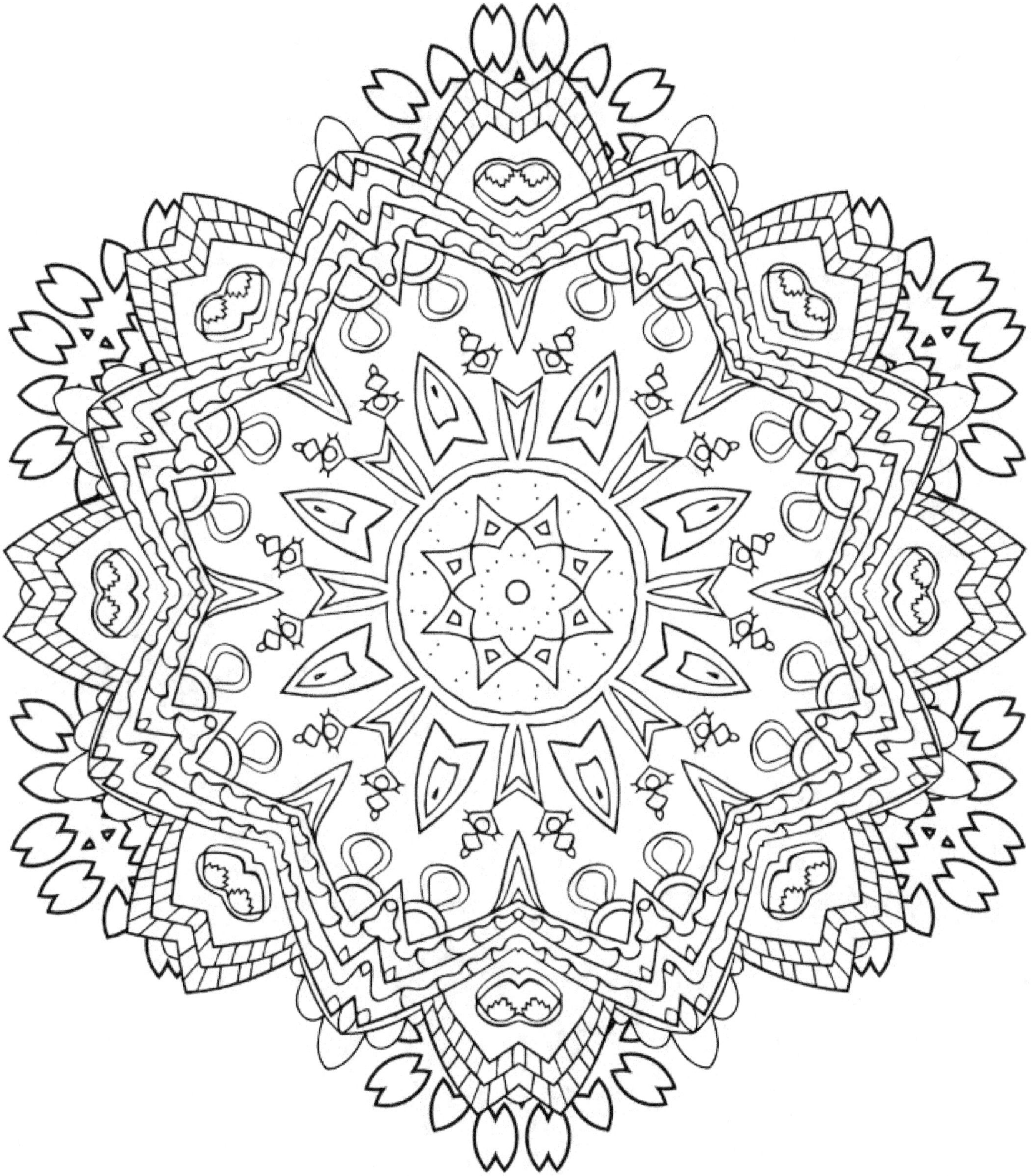

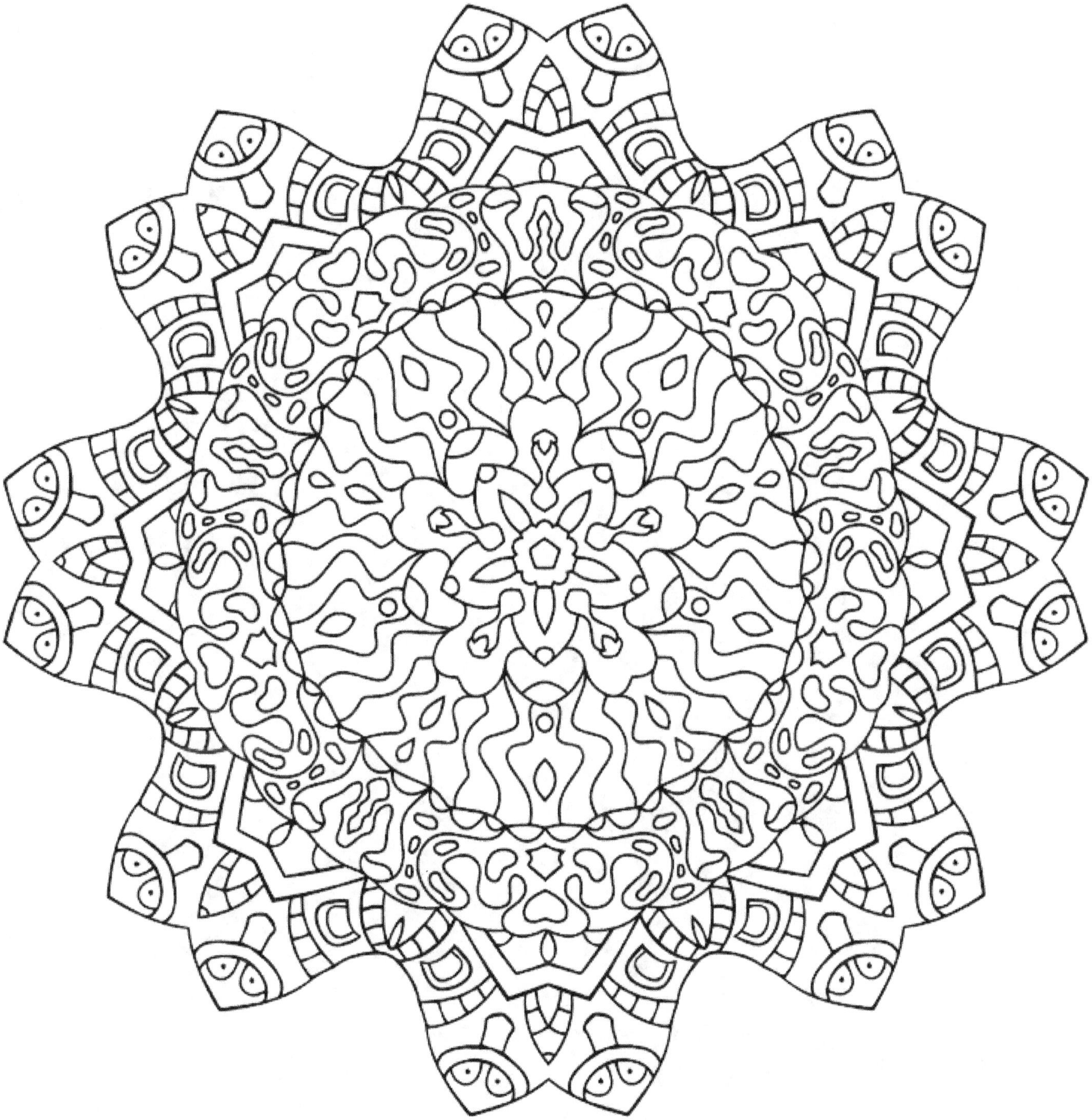

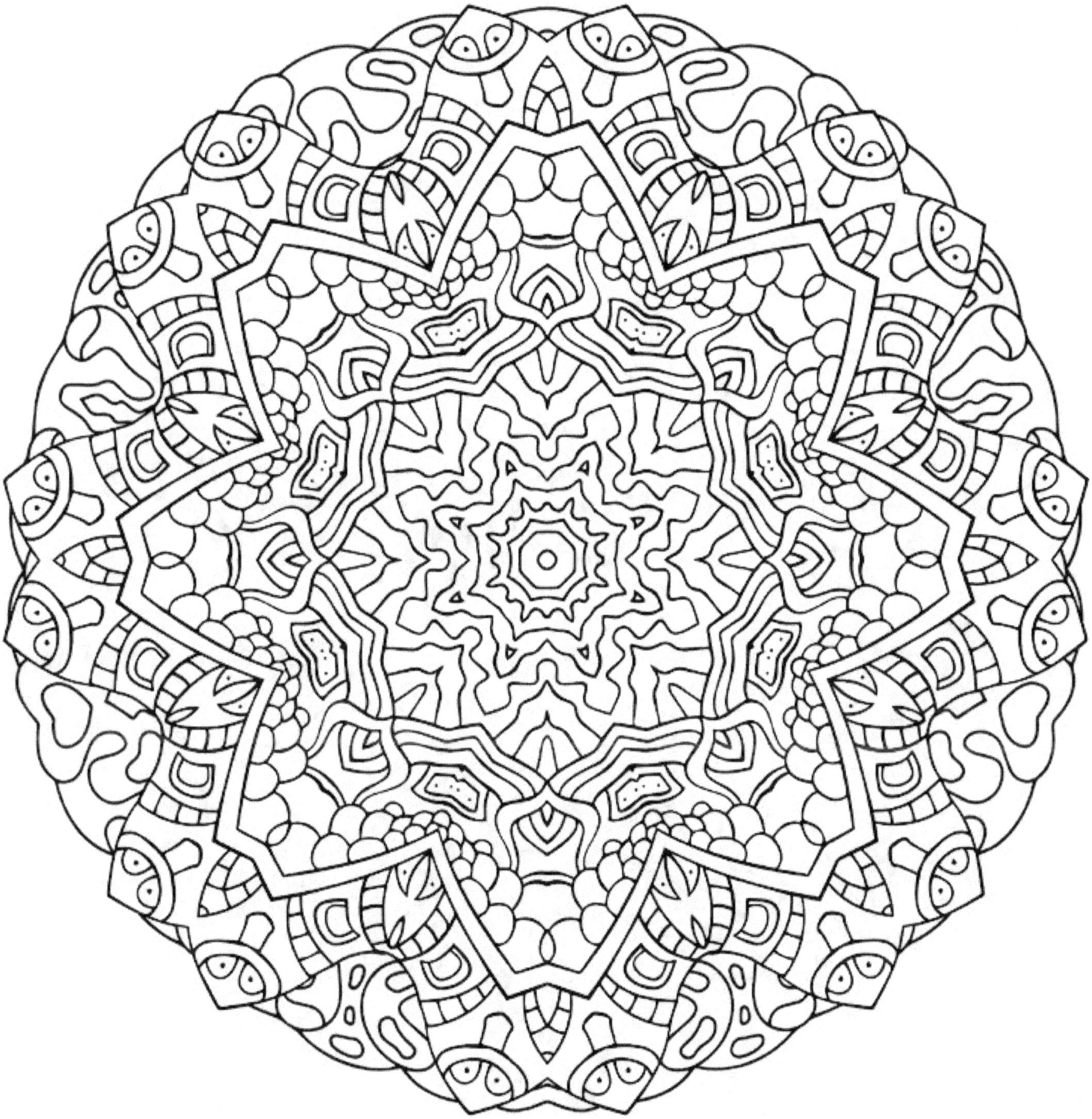

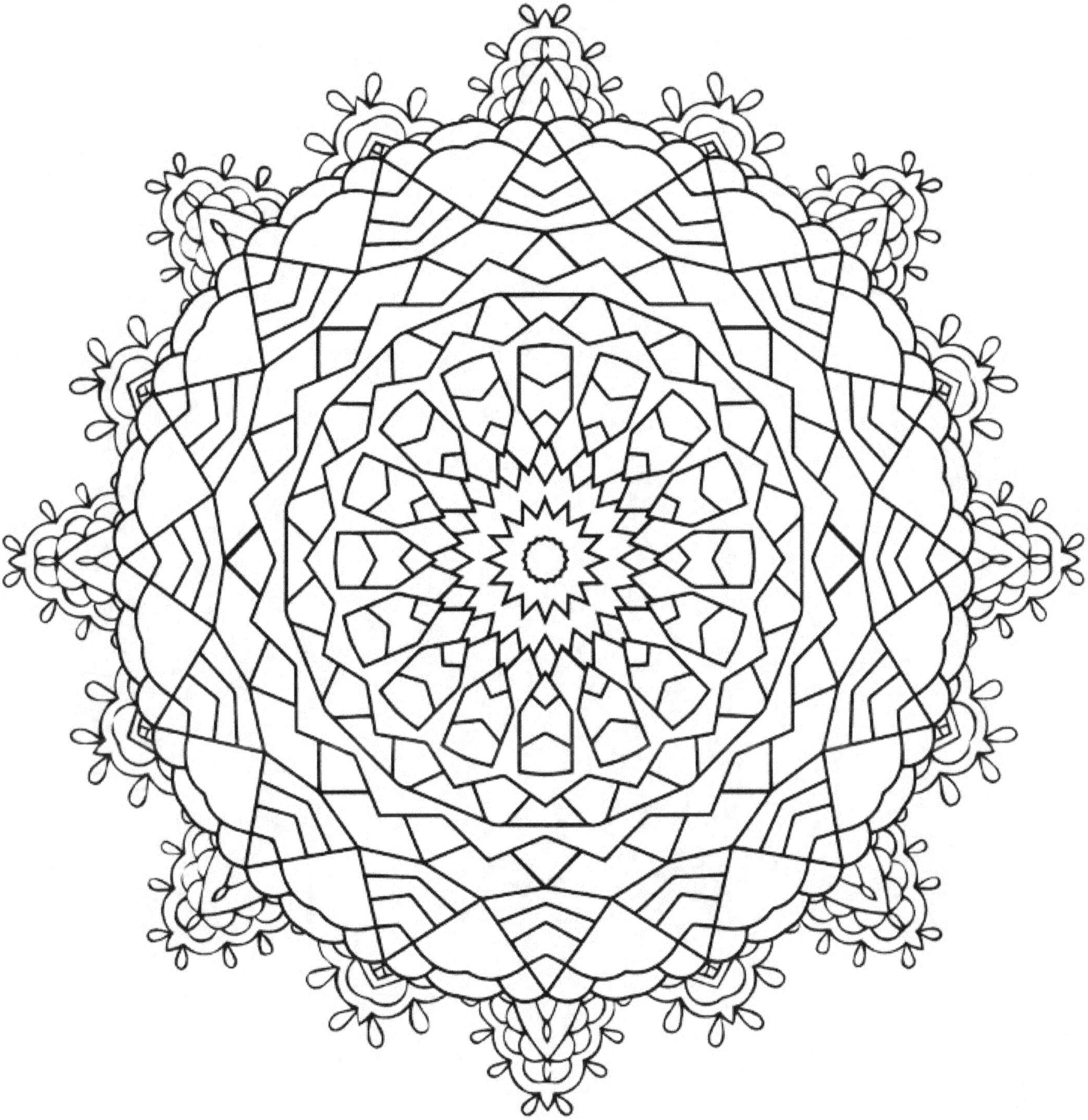

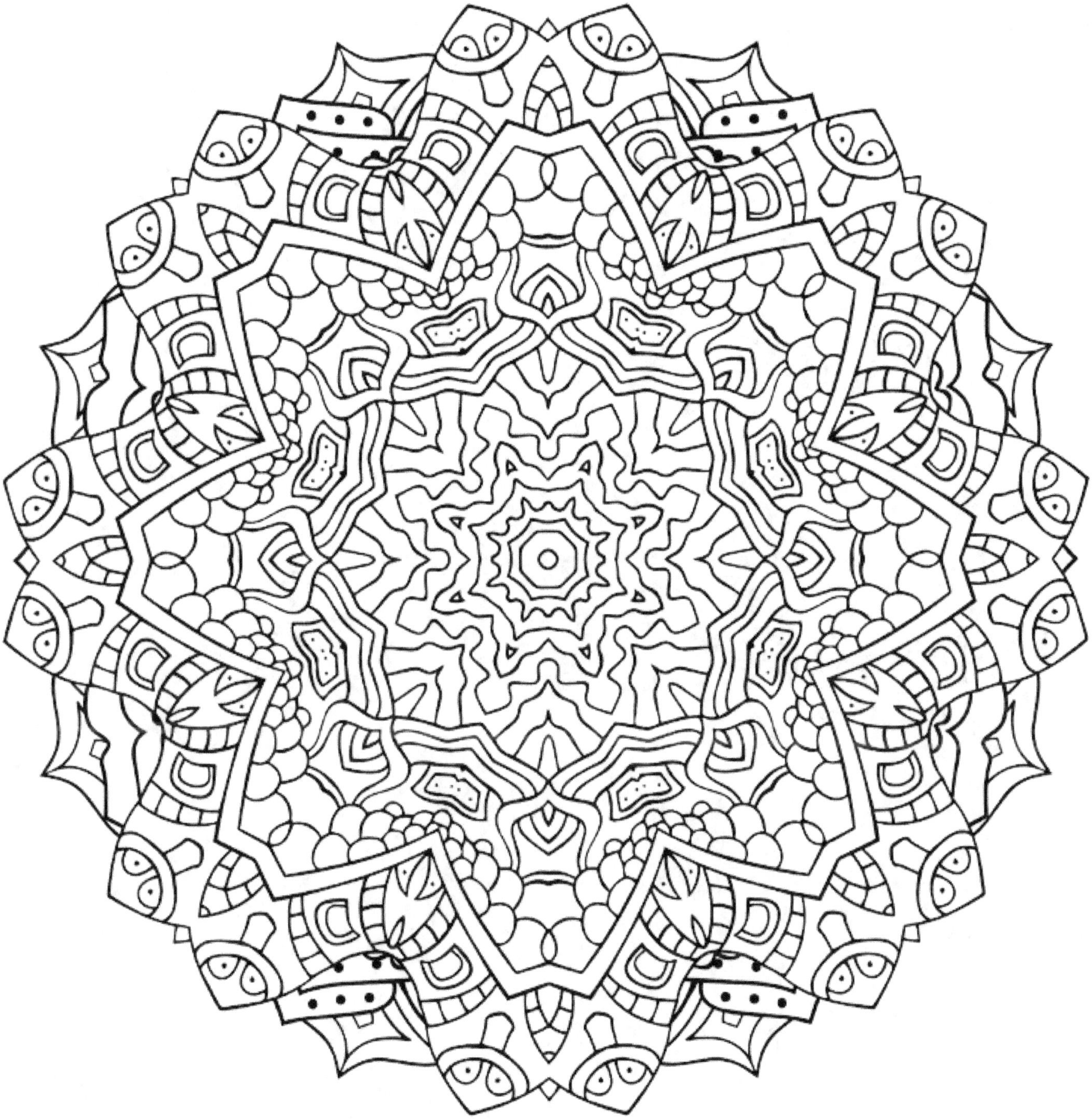

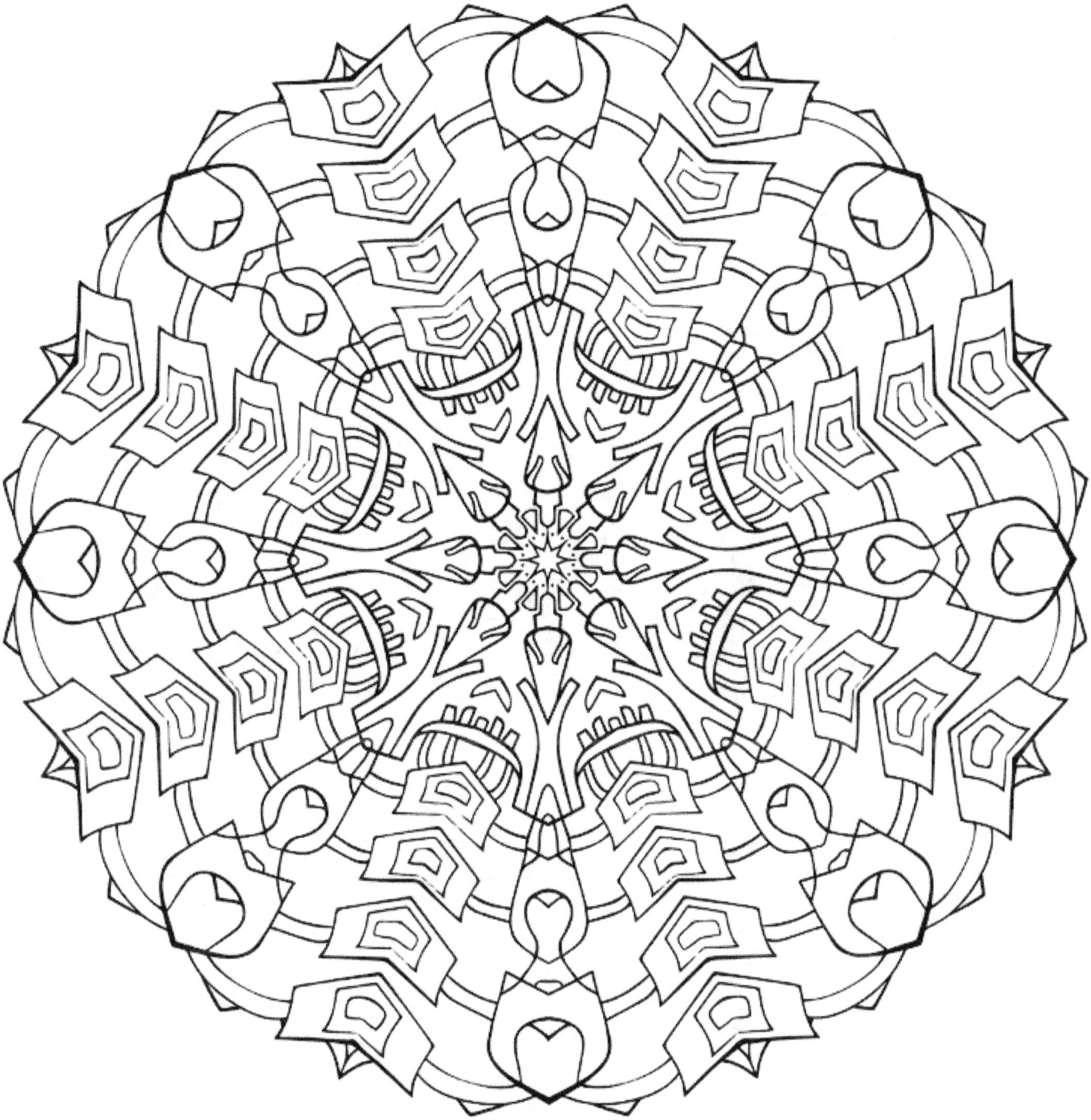

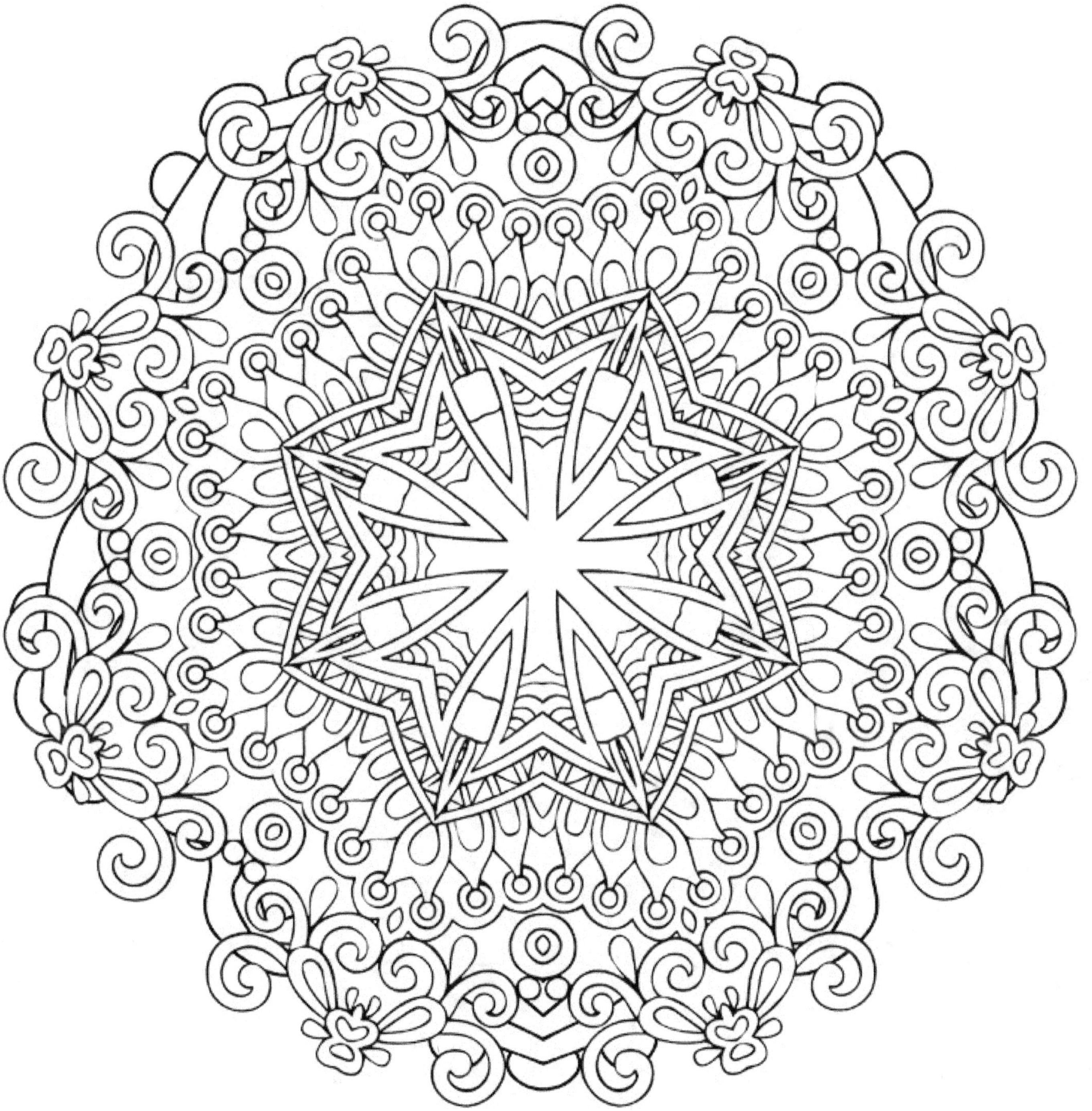

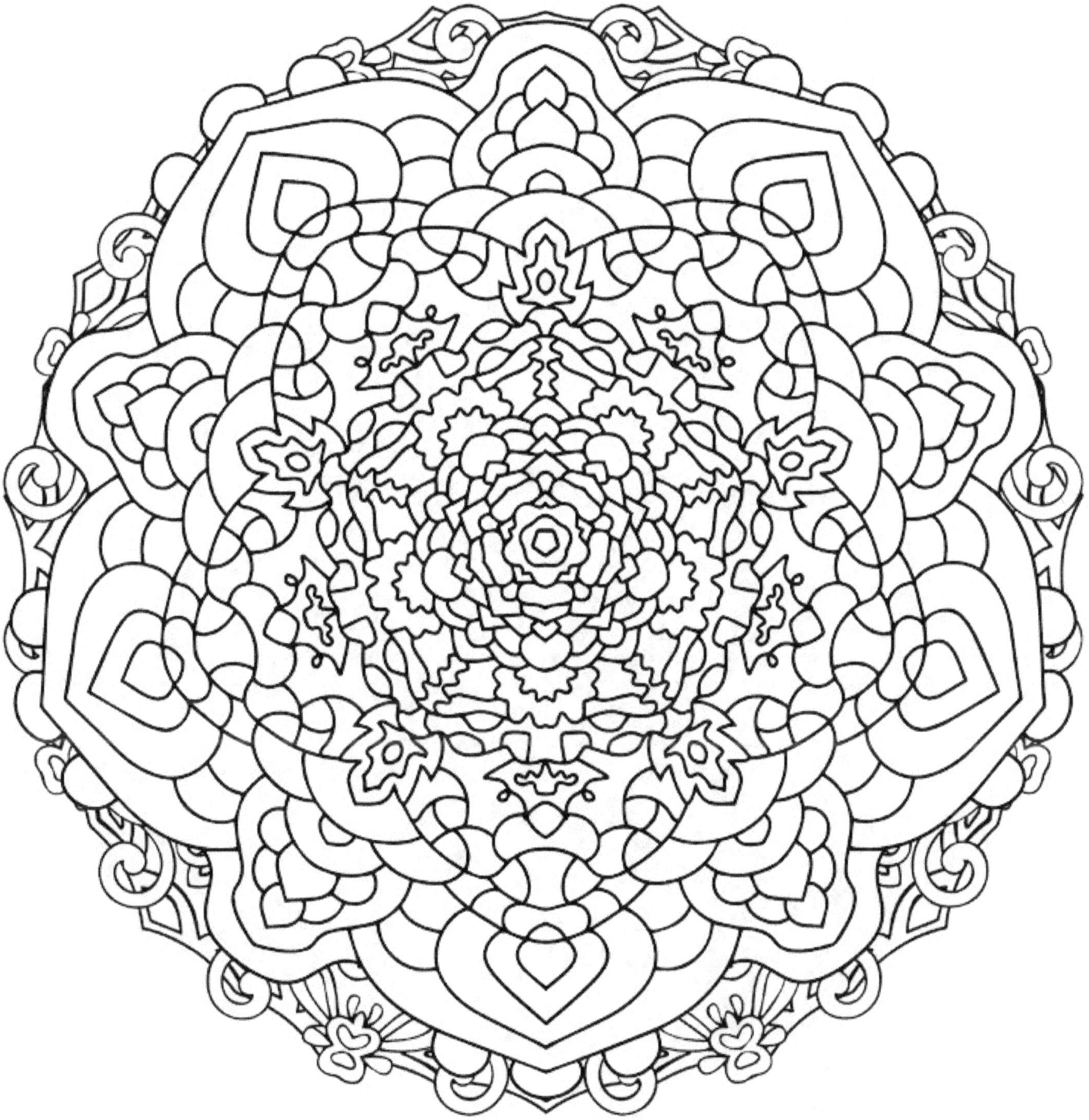

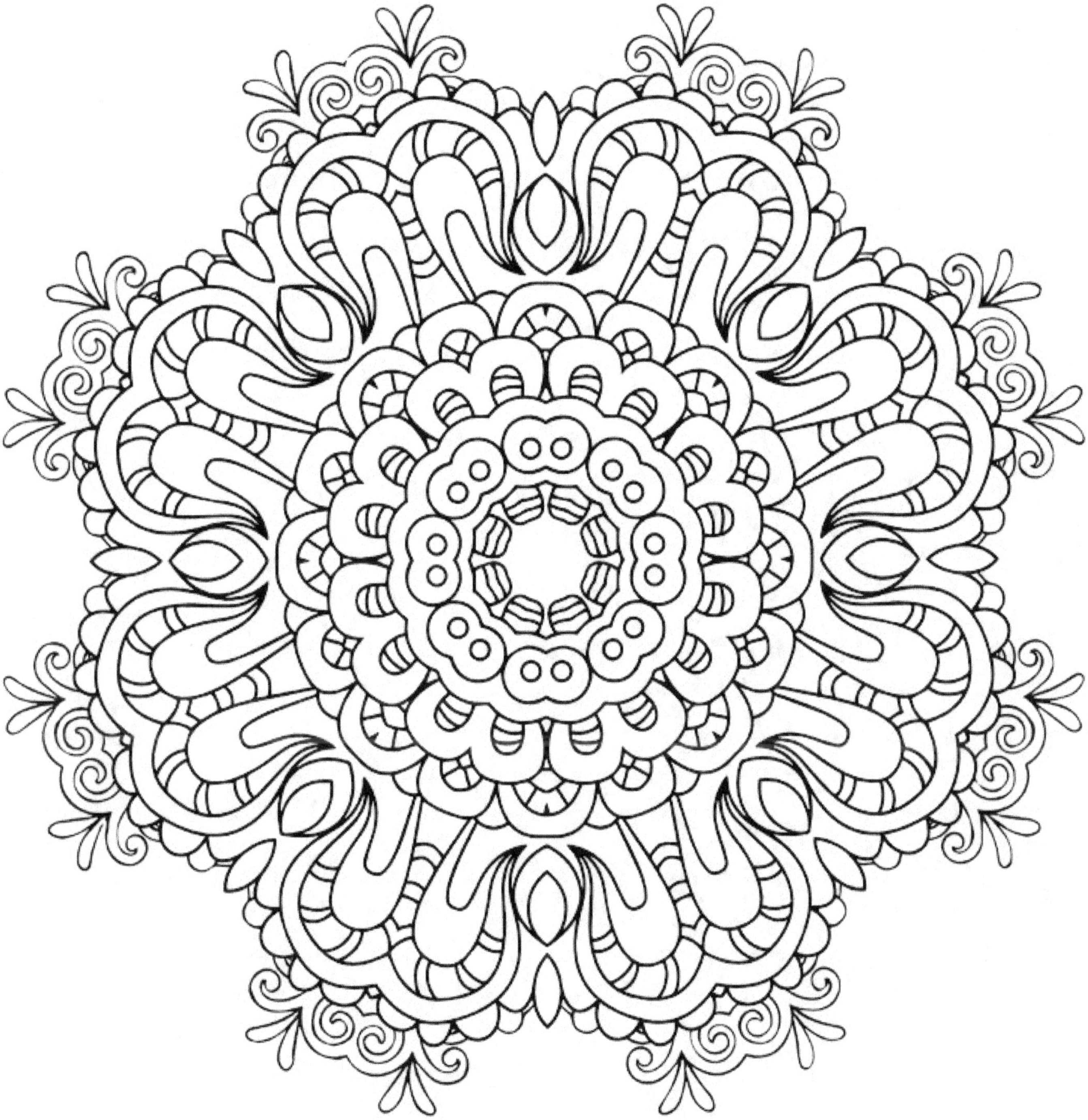

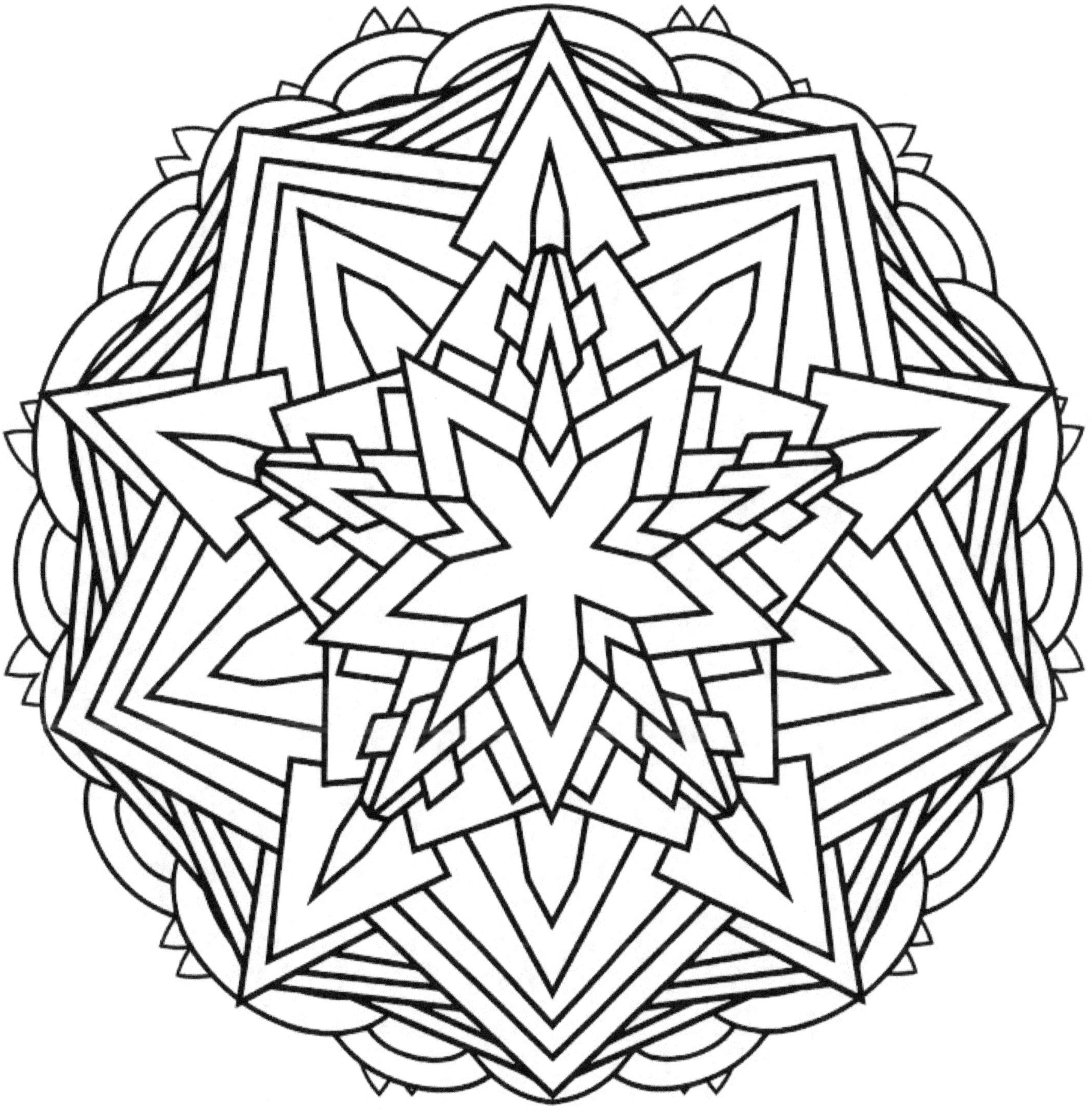

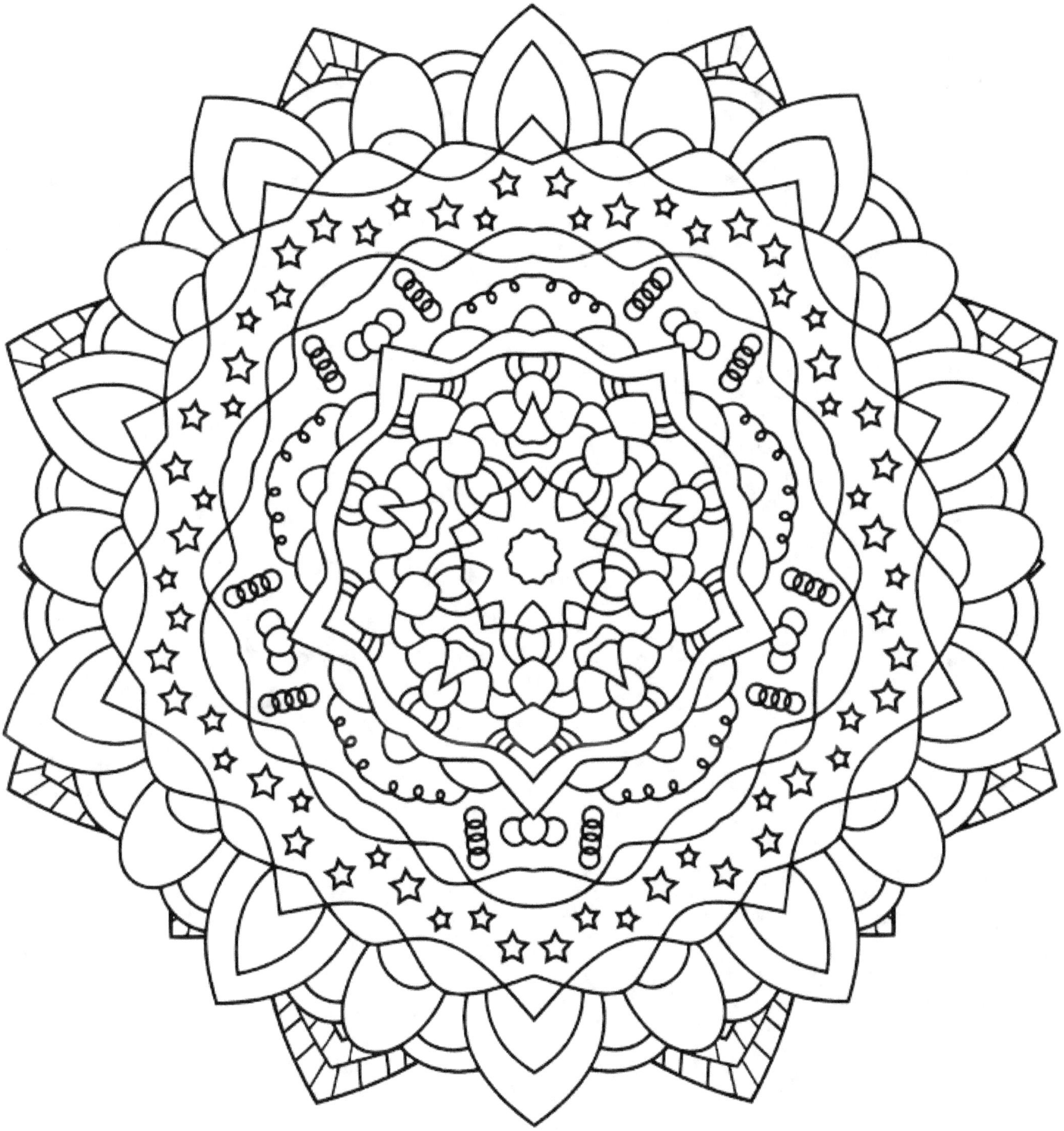

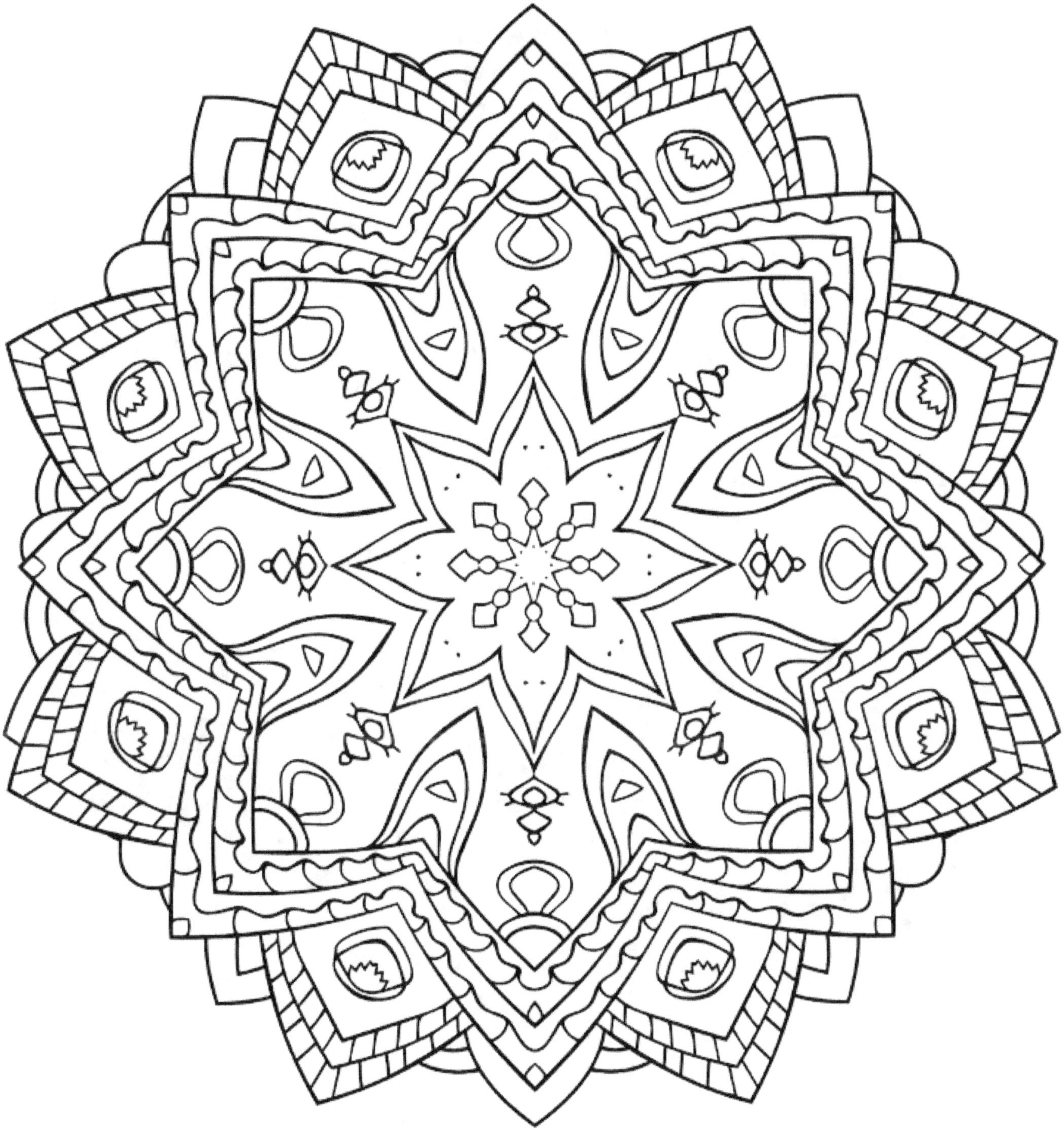

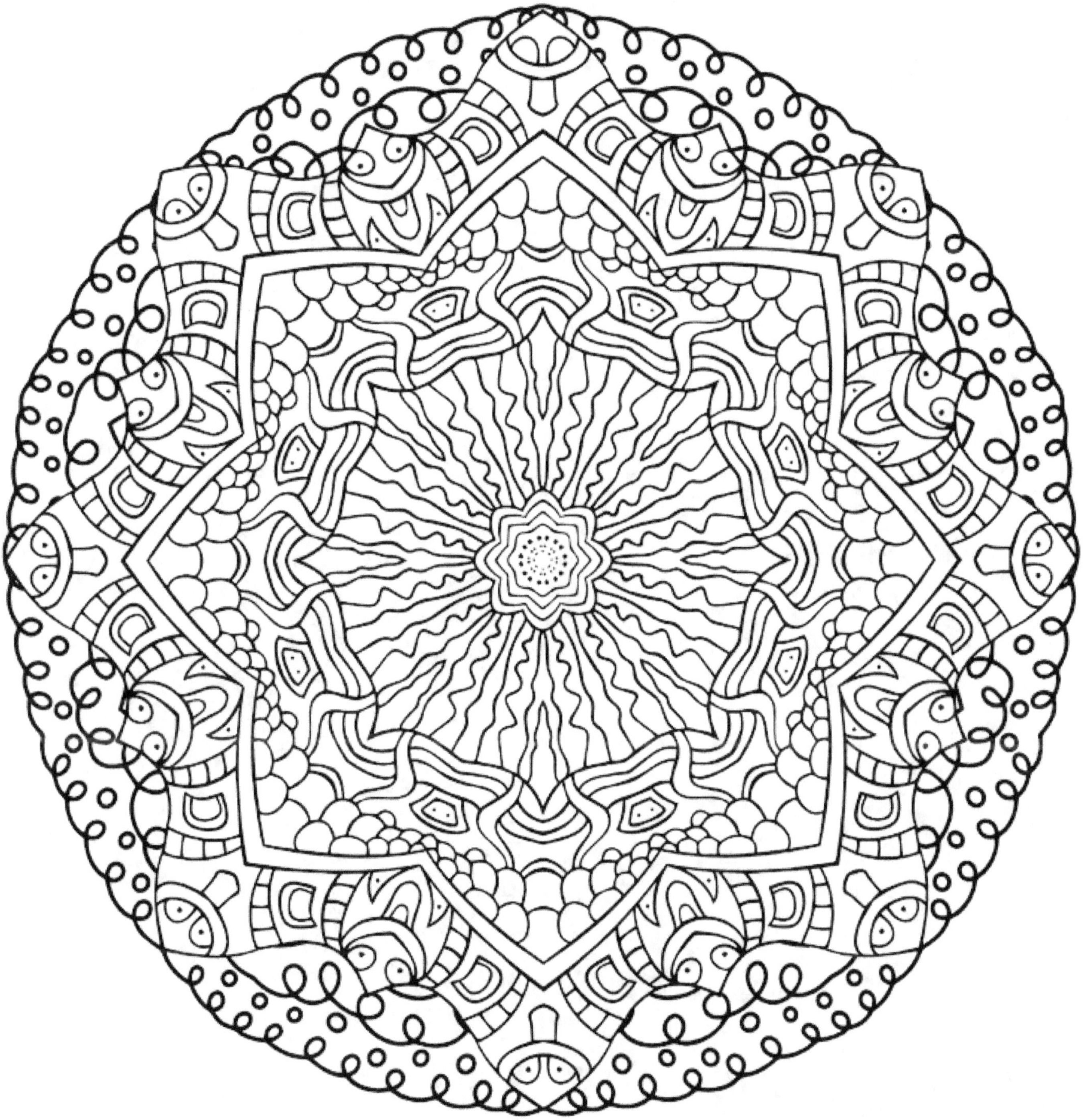

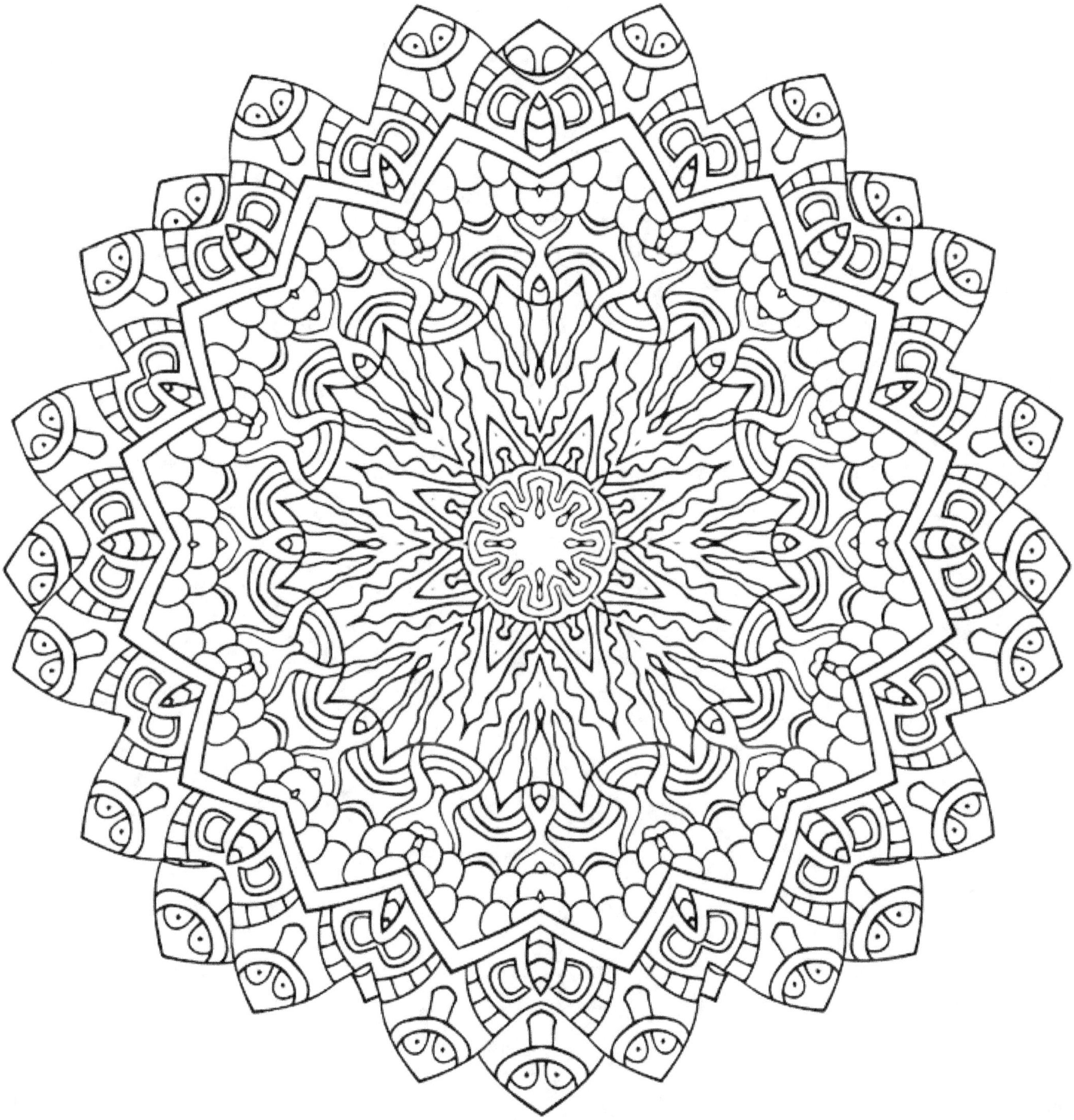

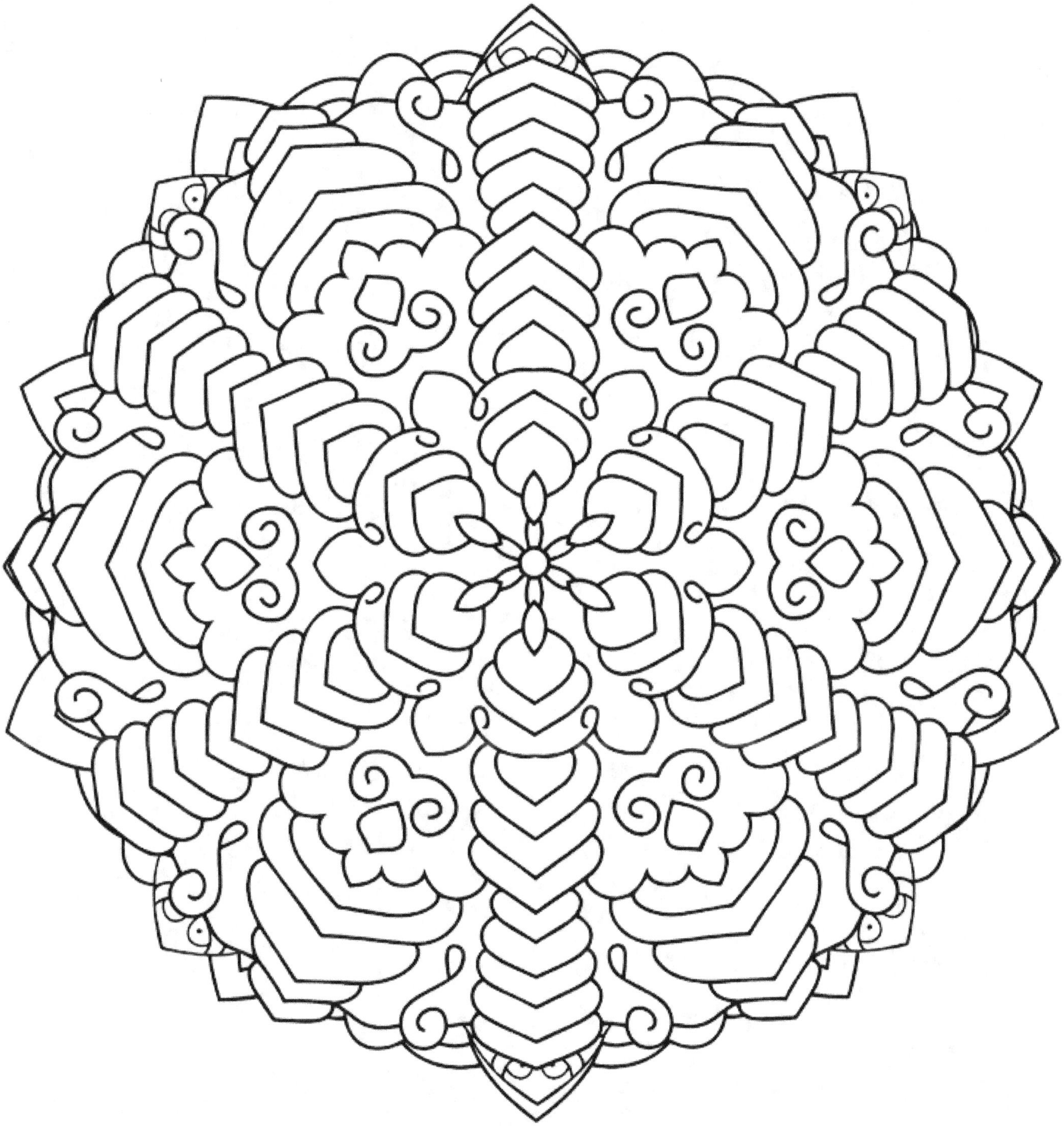

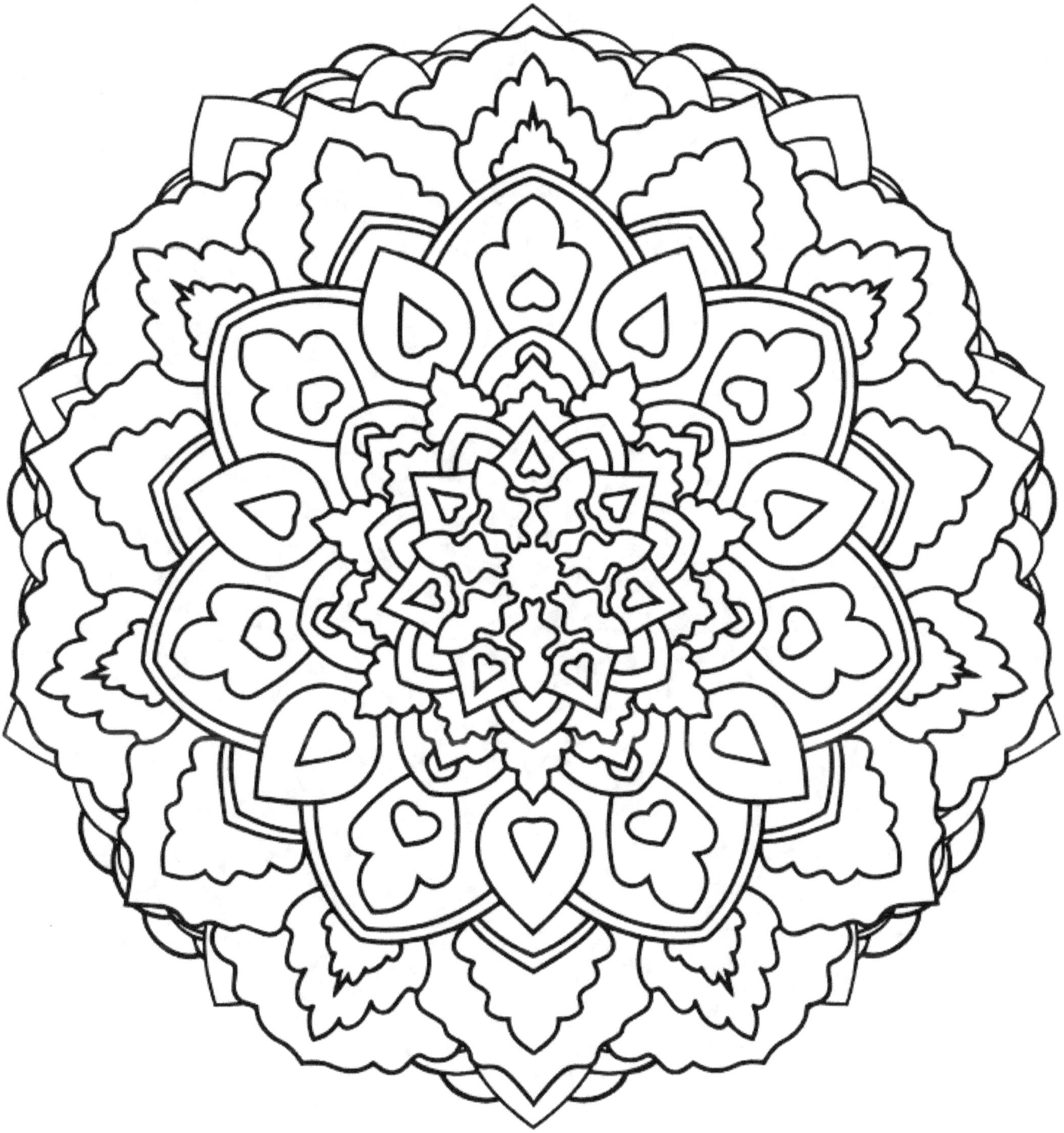

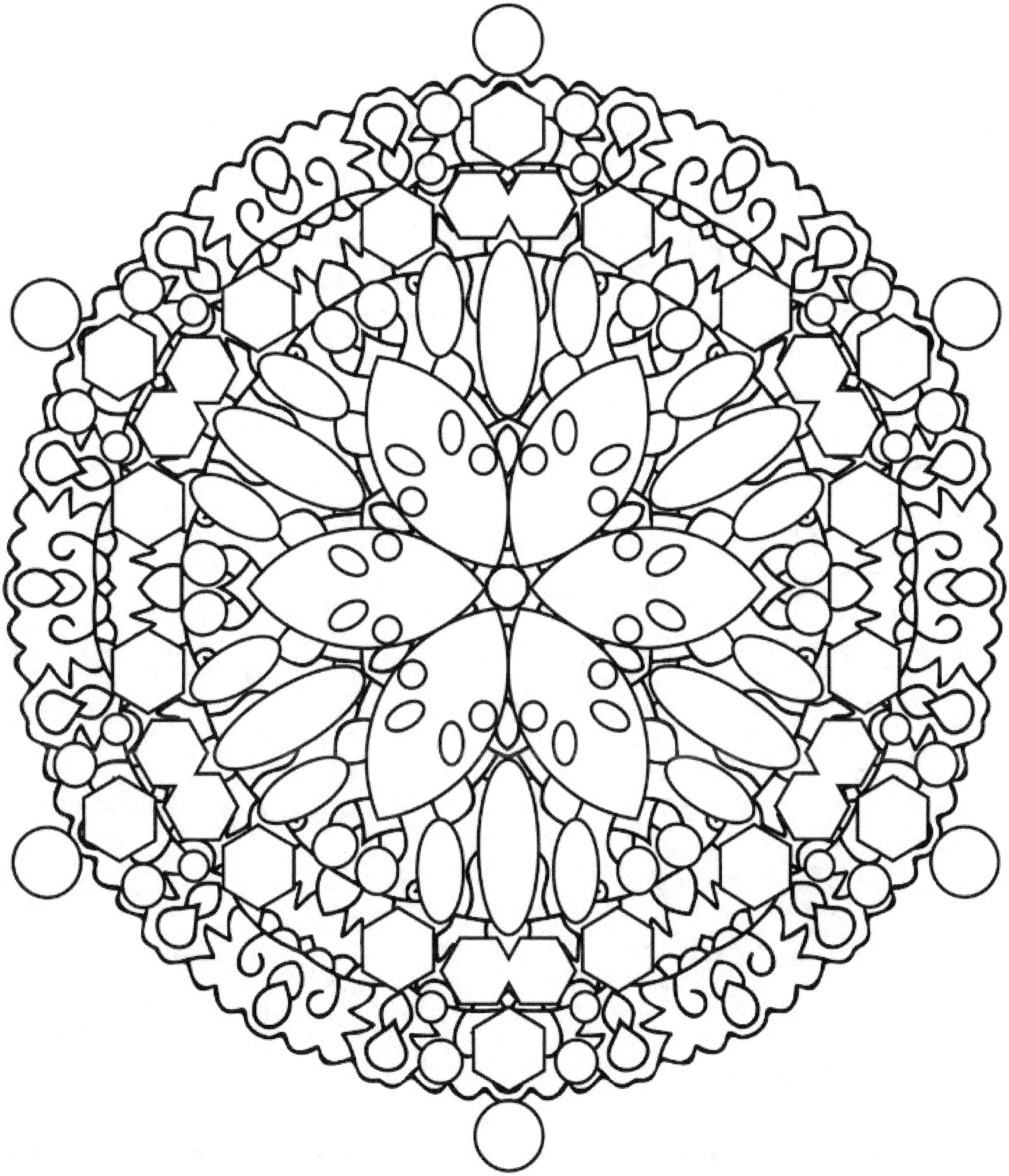

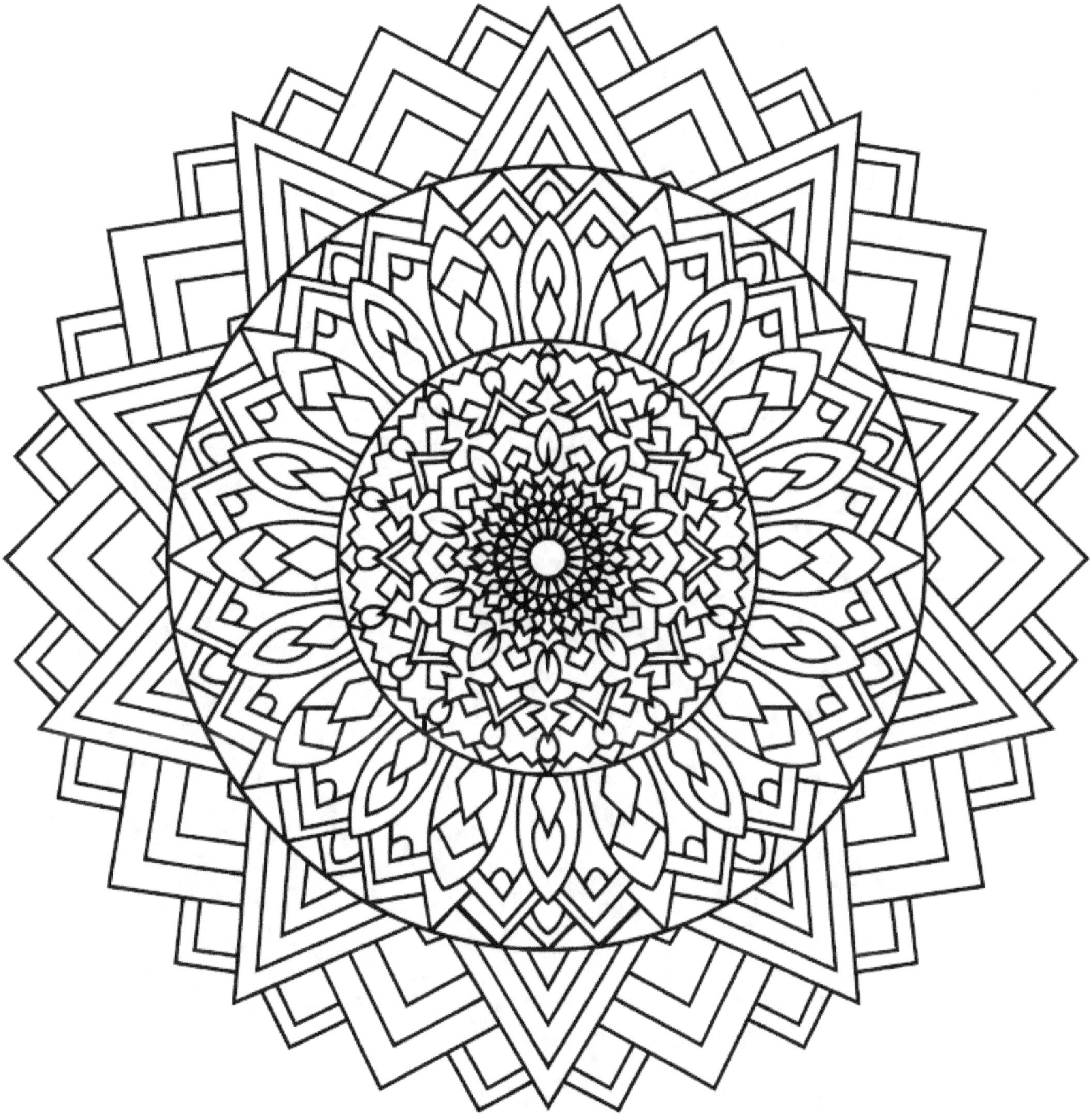

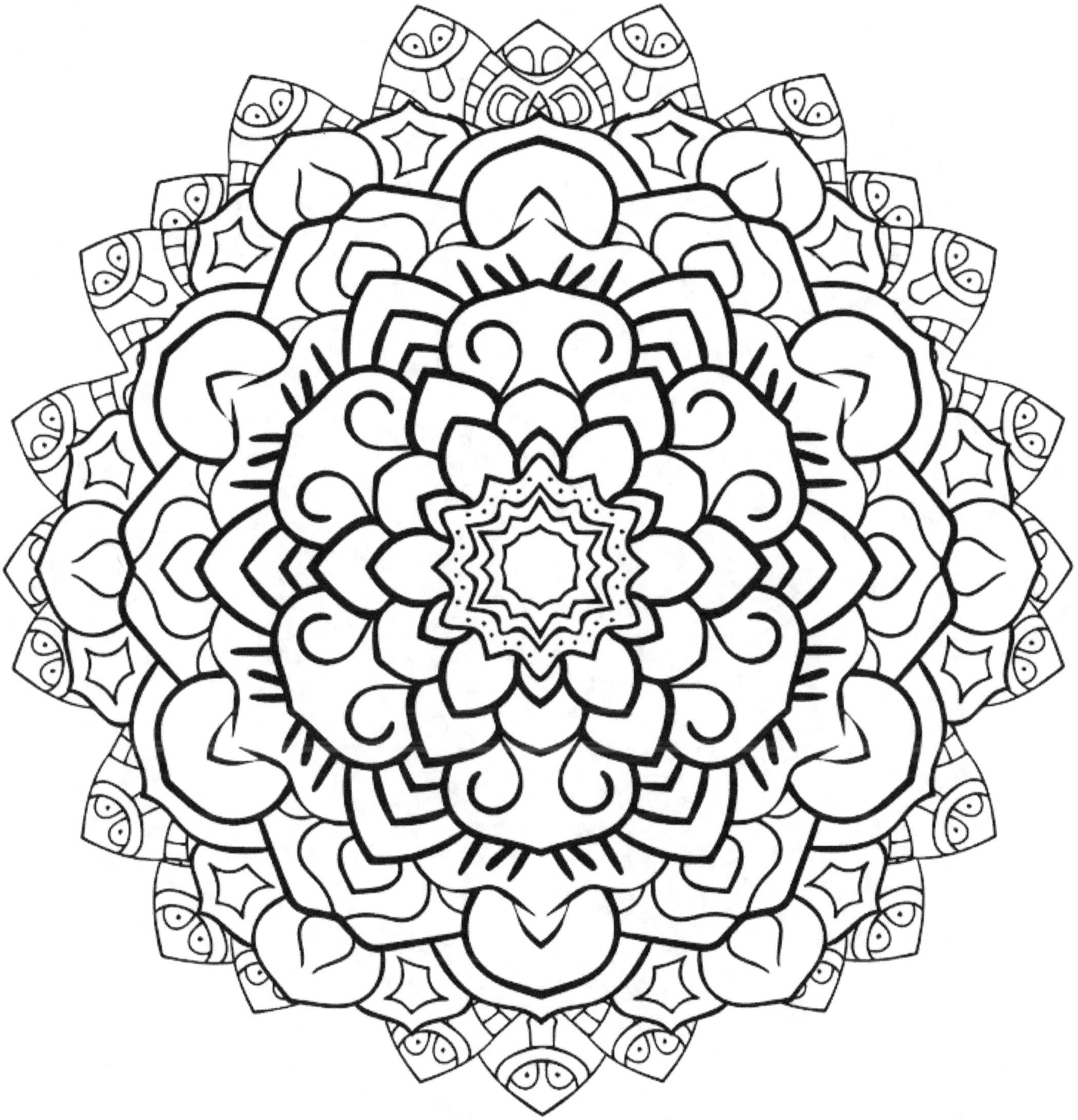

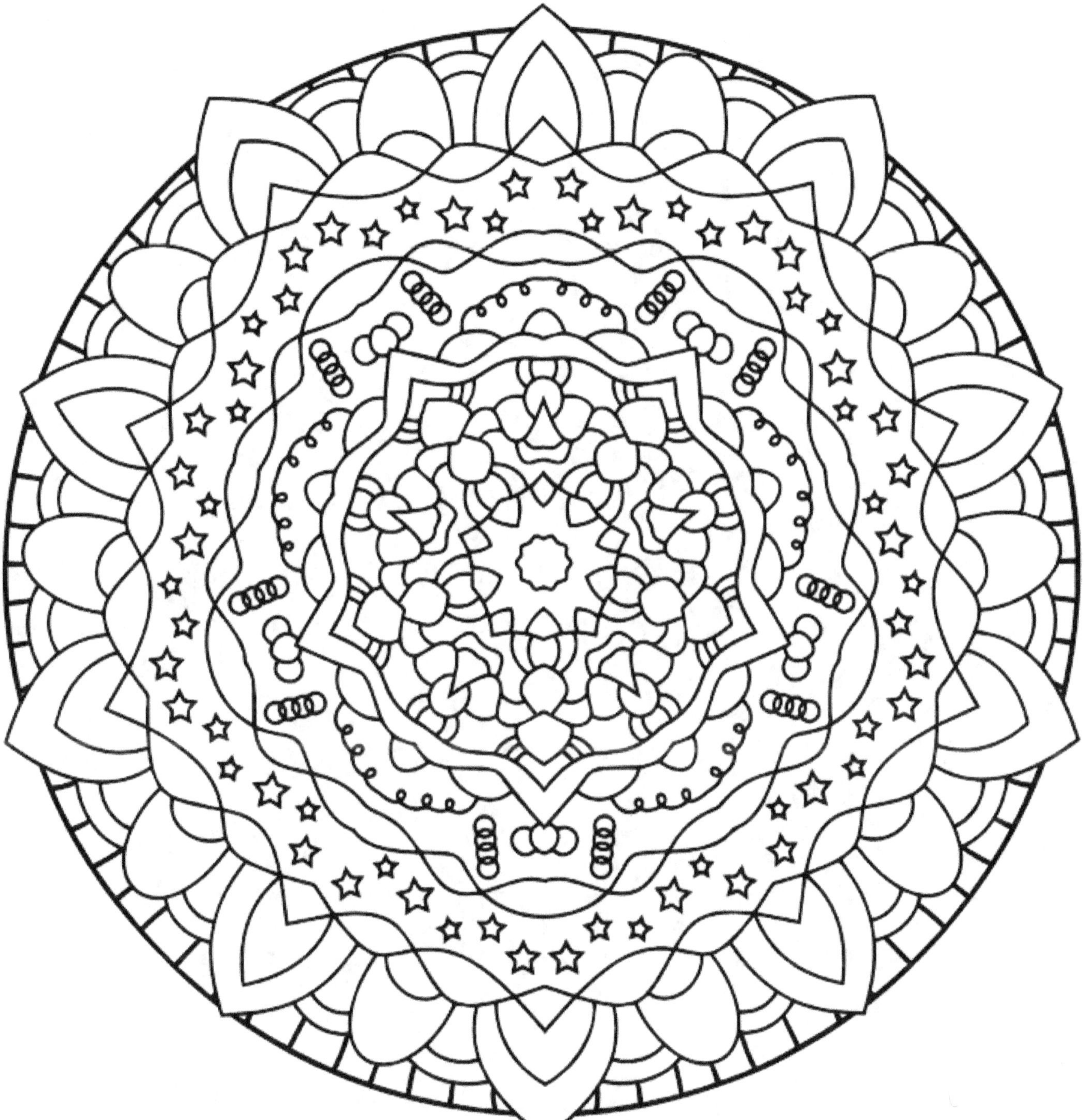

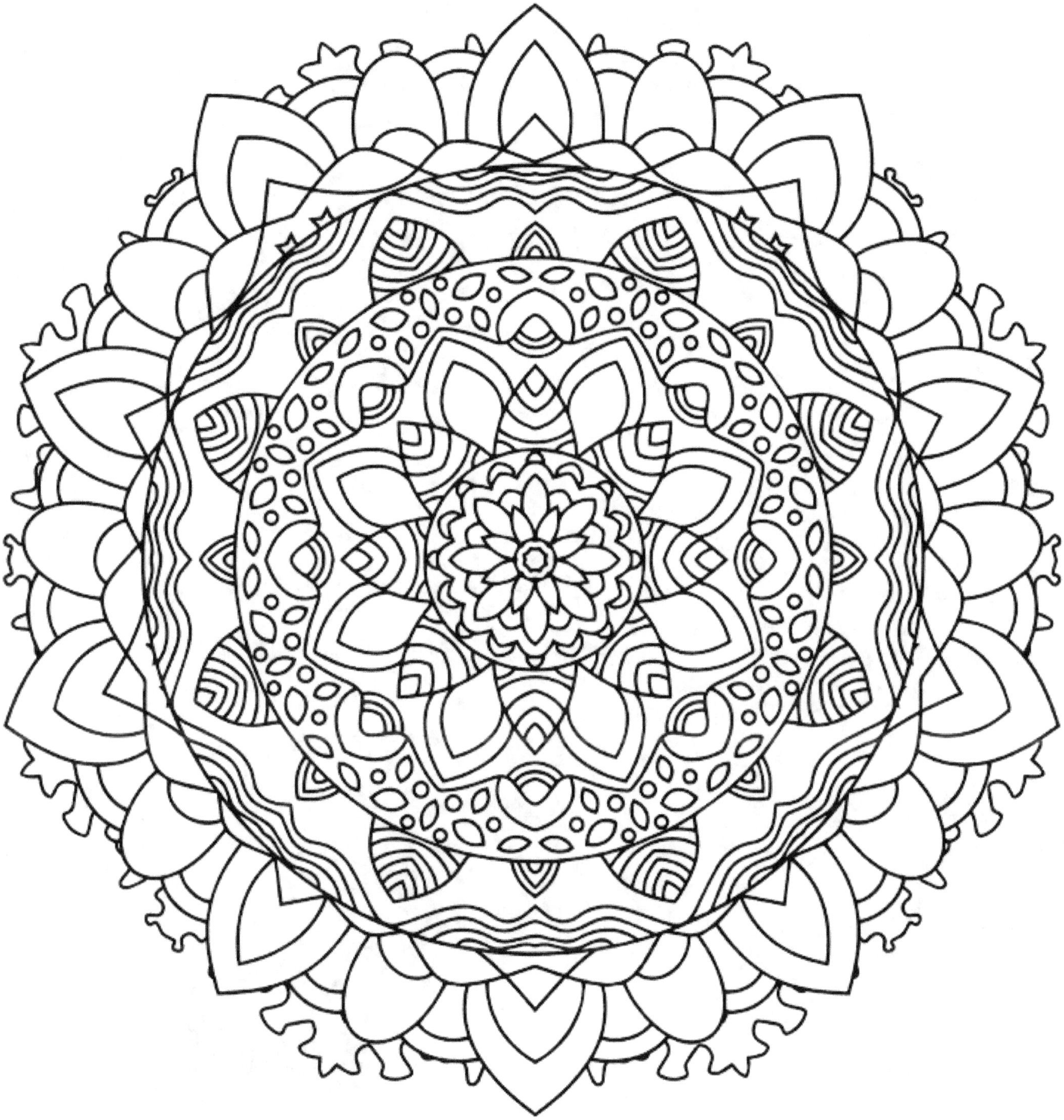

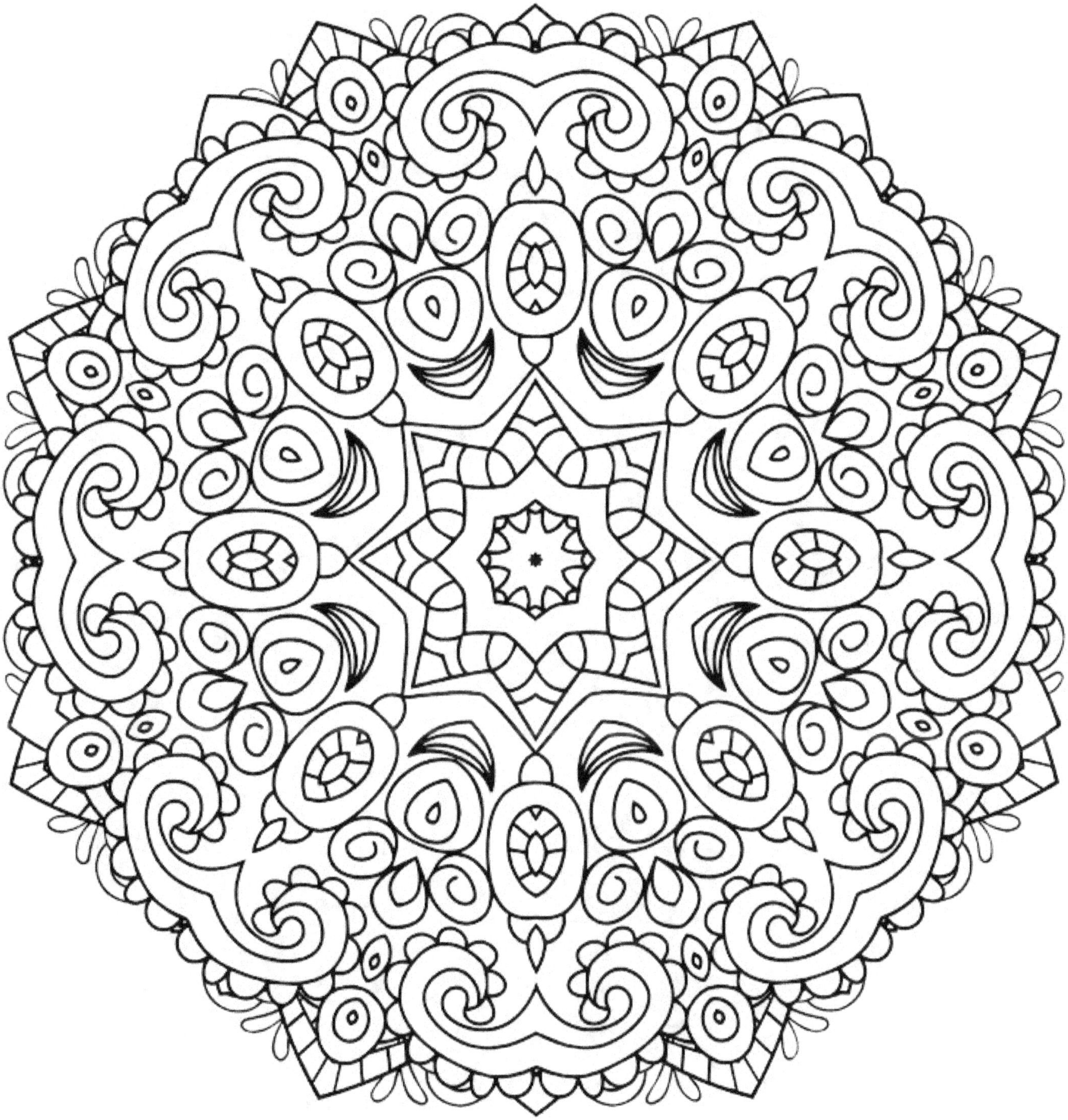

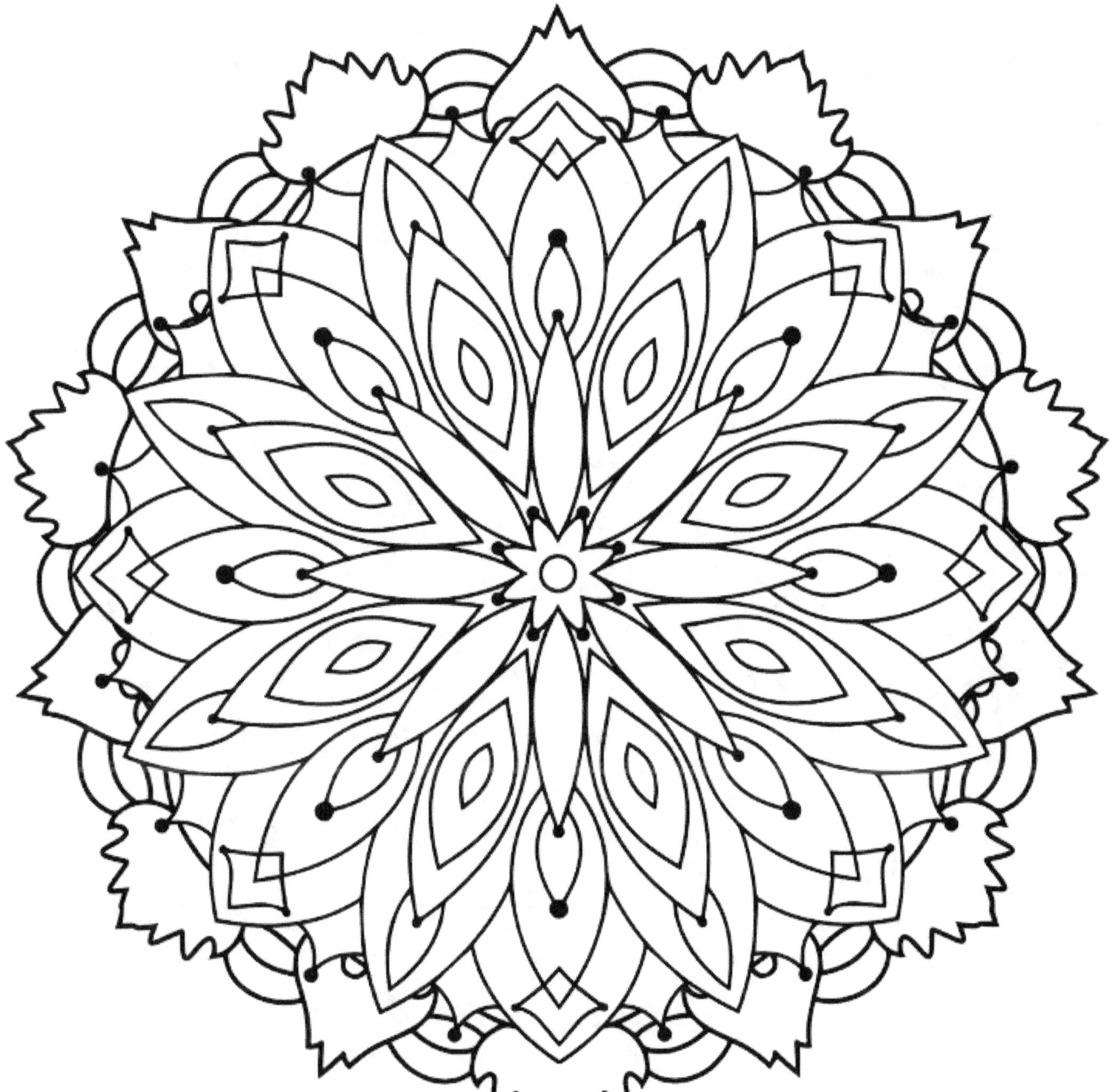

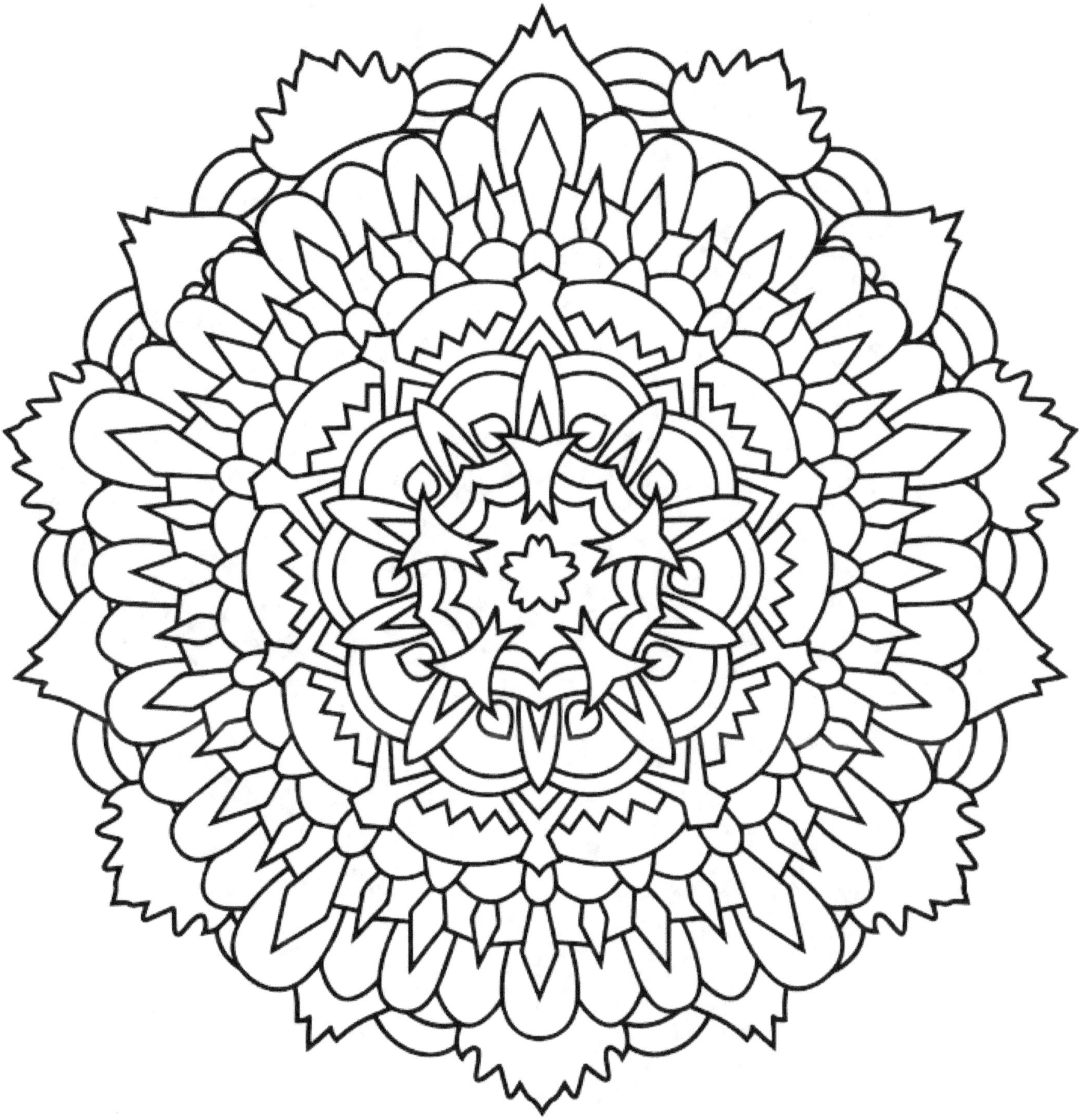

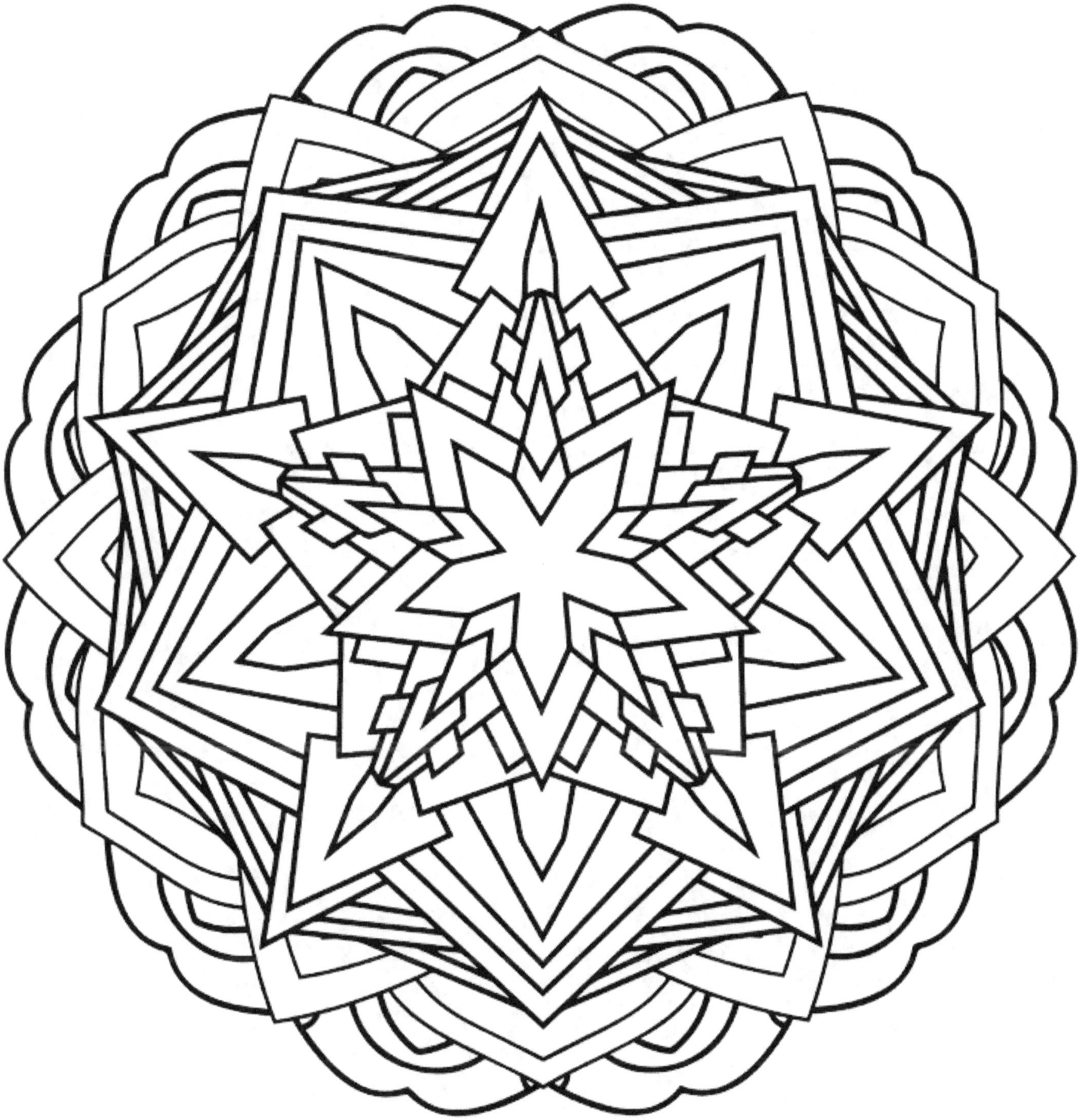

www.ingramcontent.com/pod-product-compliance
Lightning Source LLC
Chambersburg PA
CBHW080558220526
45466CB00010B/3188